# COME TO MY TABLE

### GOD'S HOSPITALITY & YOURS

## SUE MOORE DONALDSON

For my mother,

Betty Elizabeth Moore,

who invites the world to her door,

opens it wide,

and expects everyone to end up in the kitchen.

# Contents

Introduction

**Part I: Opening Your Door**

**Part II: God's Hospitality**

# Introduction

Why do we open our homes?

Isn't it too much trouble, time, work, mess, risk?

My friends mingle at my table—some new friends, some old. We sit, join hands, ask God to join in. He loves a party. Always has.

"Coffee? Tea? Scones?" (Need I ask?) "Did you try the Mexican Bread Pudding?"

The doorbell.

*Oh, good. More people! I wonder who it is . . . I love a crowd.*

I open the door wide; my friend brought a plate of cookies, a box of strawberries, and two kids. She grins. "Sorry I'm late . . ."

No big deal. Late is good when it comes to coffees. People arrive in tandem and get acquainted.

I peek outside while the door is still open, step out on the porch, cup my hands, and yell: "Is there anyone else? Do you want to come for coffee? There's room. There's strawberries . . . there's friends. There's God. Come on in. You may need to. Do come."

~~

1

Why invite? Because God invited first.

The Ultimate Host called you and me before we were born. He said: "Come on in, you are welcome here. I made you to know Me. You can know me best at My table."

His call is personal. He loved us and He called us. You may have answered. But is that all? Not even close. Because God welcomed us, we must pass along that welcome to others.

Why invite? Because the more we do, the more we are like God.

Is hospitality on your list of "How-to-Be-More-Christ-like"? Or, is it missing somehow? Christ went out of His way to welcome you. It makes sense that the more you invite, the more you look like the Inviter. Do you want to be like Jesus? Call your neighbor over for iced tea.

Why invite? Because people need you and your table.

You may be thinking, *Are you kidding? Have you seen my table? I haven't even seen it— too many papers and crumbs and books and bills. Besides, I'm no cook, I'm no Martha Stewart; and I'm not my mother—*

Are you finished? A lonely person doesn't care about crumbs. She needs Jesus. She needs a friend. She needs something to do on a Saturday evening or a Monday morning. She doesn't need gourmet, she needs a glass of water given in Jesus' name. Will you pour it? Others will come, but you do need to open your door.

Why invite? Because your faith will grow.

Obedience involves risk. But once you take the risk, faith deepens. Does God want you to invite the world? Probably not; your living room isn't that big. But He does want you to invite. Who in your world has not seen your kitchen sink? It's time. Trust Him for the courage to be His welcome to the people He puts in your path.

The more you invite, the more you understand how much God wants you next to Him at His table.

Maybe you need to start there. God invited you—do you believe that? Then it's time to pick up the phone and say, "Can you come by? I'll make coffee."

~~

# Lori's Orange Scones

Try this simple treat for morning coffee or a bracing cup of afternoon tea. Invite a neighbor in so that you aren't tempted to eat the whole batch. . .

1 ¾ cups flour

3 T. sugar

2 ½ t. baking powder

2 t. grated orange peel

Combine and cut in ⅓ cup butter until the mixture resembles fine crumbs. Stir in ½ cup raisins or dried cranberries (optional), 1 egg slightly beaten, and 4-6 T. half and half.

Turn dough out onto a lightly floured surface. Knead lightly, 10 times. Roll into a 9" circle and cut into 12 wedges. Place on a cookie sheet. Brush with a beaten egg. Bake 10-12 minutes at 400°. (It's worth keeping an orange on hand just for these!)

# Part I

# Opening Your Door

## *Prologue*

"Hey, there! Sue, I'm here! Sue? *Where is everybody?* I'm coming in . . . shall I put the kettle on?"

I could hear Grace from any corner of my house. She never knocked. Her "Hey, there" was ample, and she was always welcome.

Grace thought my front door plaque, which read "Time for Tea," was out there just for her. And she knew just where to find the cream in the refrigerator door.

Grace came on in, and I was glad. And she loved it when I'd do the same.

~~

God came right on in when He sent us His Son. He hailed us loud and clear from a cross raised high:

"Hey, there, mankind, I'm here!

"I made you because I wanted you. I redeemed you because I loved you.

You are welcome here—come to My table."

Maybe you didn't know He called. He invites you to walk right in and be His very own, and He can't wait until you accept the invitation.

Once you do, you'll know that the greatest thing you can do is to let others in on His welcome—let them know they're invited, too.

What better place to show God's welcome heart than in your own home? Go ahead, put the kettle on. God knows who's right outside and ready to knock.

# Chapter 1

# The Hosting Challenge

Depending on your background or upbringing, you either get real excited or become fainthearted, flummoxed, and fumbling when someone mentions company's coming. If the subject comes up, suddenly that appointment for a root canal sounds mildly appealing.

What can make one person delight in hospitality and another run the other way?

My friend Ceslie loves having people over to her house. In fact, she goes into a funk if she hasn't served food to someone other than her family for two weeks in a row. One birthday celebration, she invited me for lunch . . . and fifty of my closest friends. It gives her great joy to have people at her table—the more the better; the more often, the better. Every time our family comes to her house for dinner, her husband quietly thanks us because it's kept Ces from going into the depths of despair.

Ceslie loves hospitality in part because she was raised that way. Her Mama Marian was a great example to her, and she passed on that "open home" heritage in abundance. Not everyone is raised by a Mama Marian. And that can make all the difference.

But upbringing is only one consideration. What else can keep us from opening our door? I've found that there are many other reasons why we aren't hospitable (when we aren't.)

The very thought of inviting people to your house can raise practical issues and questions like:

Whom should I invite? How will I fit everyone around my table?

How will I fit this into my already packed schedule?

What will I serve? What if they don't like the food? I'm not really a cook.

How will I pay for it? I'm on a tight enough budget as it is.

What if they don't want to be invited?

Should I get new carpeting first?

These are all valid questions—some more than others.

I asked a group of ladies why they don't have people over (when they don't), and here are some of their answers. Maybe you can relate to one of them:

1. *"Hospitality wasn't modeled for me in my upbringing, so I don't have any experience."* (Your mom didn't do it, so you don't know where to begin.)

2. *"I'm afraid I won't do it 'right'—I don't want to appear ignorant or foolish."*

(No one likes to feel awkward, as if they don't know what they're doing, even if the guest doesn't seem to care or even notice.)

3. *"What if my things (food? furniture? dishes?) are not good enough for company?"* (I call this the "Martha Stewart Syndrome." Americans have been handed a standard of finesse that is fine for entertaining but has nothing to do with hospitality.)

4. *"My expectations can be too high."* (My sister Lori said that sometimes her own expectations have kept her from making the effort. For example, she might have wanted to prepare appetizers to serve on the deck before dinner, as well as make her favorite homemade lemon meringue pie. But since she couldn't do it all on a particular day—she has four kids—she wouldn't want to do it at all.)

5. *"I think it's just too much work (and I'm too tired)!"* (Our homes might be in the "can't-have-anyone-over syndrome." It's too much work to prepare; too much work to clean up.)

6. *"I'm too shy. What would I talk about? Do we have enough in common? Couldn't it turn out to be awkward for everyone?"* (This attitude says, "It's okay for the extrovert to be hospitable, but it's way out of my comfort zone. Let someone else do it.")

7. *"I think my house is too small."* (This is a common response. Maybe you don't have enough chairs. Is the couch too shabby? I just took a better look at our couch this week and realized I'll need to cover it with all my afghans sewn together so I can keep inviting people to come in; or I could just stop having company. Maybe your living room does double or triple duty as the playroom, the dining room, or the study and office, so you're waiting for your next house [or the next couch]. This could be the "waiting-for-things-to-get better" syndrome.)

8. *"It's just too inconvenient."* (Perhaps your guests are the neighbor kids, and you've just mopped the floors; or your in-laws called, and you just got over Christmas. Guests may stay too long and interfere with your family's normal routine.)

Can you identify with any of these eight reasons? Maybe the list made you think of another reason that keeps your hand off the phone and your house to yourself. I know that any one or a combination of the above could make me stop hosting altogether. After all, that couch is a wreck, and after a busy week, I can feel as shabby as that wingback chair that desperately needs to be recovered.

Think about it. Do any of the reasons on this list have to do with putting the guest and the relationship first? I don't think so. Each one has to do with self, with a capital "S"! When I looked at the list, I placed the letter "P" by each reason that might have to do with PRIDE. They all got "P's."

*Pride* goes hand in hand with *fear*, because pride has to do with depending on yourself instead of on God. *Pride* and *fear* immobilize us—we fear failure, what others might think, appearing inept. So, we don't invite anyone over, and it all has to do with thinking of self instead of extending the welcome of God's heart.

The great thing about showing others God's welcome is that we are not alone in our efforts. God doesn't expect us to do this all by ourselves. He gives us grace and strength when we ask Him. He forgives our pride. He provides the strength to host in spite of our valid and invalid reasons.

God told us in the Bible, "Be hospitable" (Hebrews 13:2). He wouldn't tell us that without promising to help. It's not about us, as they say; it's about Him and people who need to meet Him while at your table. If you and I remember that we are not inviting people over to show off our skills or homes, but rather to serve our guests, we can more readily offer God' welcome, with or without a new carpet.

## The Differences Between Hospitality and Entertaining

Last week at work, a colleague said to me, "So, you give tea parties?" It sounded like a challenge. In case she thought I did them for a living, I started to explain, but she didn't give me a chance. She just stated simply, "I can't do that."

I was surprised. Jody seemed the perfect type of hostess—warm and engaging, personable and down-to-earth. "Anyone can do it, Jody," responded. "You just need a mug and a tea bag." She smiled. I could tell she didn't believe me.

Hospitality can seem difficult—impossible even—simply because we have the wrong idea. We've been fooled into thinking that hospitality and entertaining are the same. Both are great; and both can be used by God. But they are not the same.

The difference is *focus* and *purpose*. Unlike hospitality, the focus of entertaining is often the host rather than the guest. And the purpose of entertaining often is to impress others rather than to serve them. Once you understand these differences, you can begin to feel the freedom of welcoming the world to your door.

We've all been to the perfect party. I attended one the other night. I thoroughly enjoyed it! The home shimmered with candlelight, the gourmet food wafted its seasonal fragrance throughout each room, and I ate with relish and delight. It was practically perfect in every way—actually, it was perfect— the way it looked, the way it smelled, the way it tasted. *Southern Living* photo shoots never had it so good! The evening was truly a work of art.

What my host did was entertain, and she did it with flair and beauty. But is that what is meant by hospitality—showing God's welcoming heart to others? If I thought so, I might never have anyone over again. My house will never look that beautiful; I can cook, but not quite like my darling hostess; and I doubt if I would take the time to carve out the mini-pumpkins for individual servings of rice pilaf.

Entertaining can portray an experienced hostess, showcasing her ability to get things right, at least for a few hours, with a relaxed and good-natured attitude. Her home is immaculate, her food is delectable, her children well behaved. "The perfect hostess!" her friends exclaim, and they don't even attempt to compete.

Does that make entertaining a less-than-worthwhile endeavor? I don't think so. God is the Author of beauty and art; some people love entertaining for art's sake, and the guests benefit as well! The artistic host is motivated to design the perfect setting or the most scintillating atmosphere. The taste of the food and how it's presented, right down to colors and textures, gives them great creative pleasure. Others love the opportunity to throw a good party where everyone goes home happy and suitably impressed. ("Where does he come up with those good ideas?")

However, great food, good times, a gorgeous home—is that what hospitality is all about?

If so, it can be far more pressure than most people want to add to their lives. No wonder couples these days would rather get a sitter and meet at a favorite restaurant, if they can afford it. With such high expectations on the host, only the most intrepid and confident person would dare send out the perfect invitation to the perfect party. Most cry, "Too much work, too much pressure, it's not worth it!" I would agree.

Magazines and television networks do their best to place hospitality and entertaining in the same camp. Just glancing at the beautiful magazine covers at the checkout stand can make you decide to not even attempt to have someone over to your home.

However, when you see clearly just how different hospitality and entertaining are, you can begin to take steps towards being hospitable the way God intended.

## The Hospitable Heart

What are the main differences? First of all, in contrast to image-conscious entertaining, true hospitality focuses on the guest rather than on the host.

- What is the person's need?

- How can you serve, comfort or accommodate this person?

- Does he or she need a place to stay or just a listening ear?

- Does he or she need a bowl of soup or just a cup of water?

Hospitality doesn't require perfection. It can happen when there's laundry on the couch and dishes in the sink. It can happen around a noisy table with macaroni and cheese as the main dish, and ice cream for dessert. My sister Lori says, "Almost anyone can serve a bowl of ice cream." And she's right.

I met a lovely young woman who was new at our church. She needed to meet some friends. However, my husband had begun a worthy but messy project in our front room—hot-gluing a giant wooden dollhouse for our middle daughter. Wood chips and rearranged furniture aside, I had some ladies over for coffee so she could begin to feel at home in our fellowship. Solana commented to me as she was leaving, "I'm so glad to be in someone's home that isn't perfect. It makes me feel normal." I'm afraid my home is always "normal," in that sense; I just had a good excuse for the mess this time. But, she was right. And I was glad I had made the effort for her sake.

We've been fooled into thinking that hospitality has to do with us—the host—rather than the one who needs a place at our table.

The word "hospitality" comes from the Latin root *hostis*, which means "enemy or stranger." Obviously way back when, hospitality had nothing to do with a grand event for your best friends. In ancient days, a hospital was a place of shelter for the traveler, who could very likely have been a stranger, or even an enemy. The chief purpose of a "hospitaler" was to care for the sick and needy, whether friend or foe.

The focus of true hospitality is your guest. Who could benefit by a visit to your home and a seat at your table? Is it someone you know well or someone you've just met? That person could very well be a stranger, maybe even someone who doesn't think or act or look like you do. What is the best way to serve her?

If I were to take a word-association test for the word "hospitality," I might say: "Milk and cookies"

"Milk and cookies" creates an image of warmth and fullness, welcome and preparation, expectation and caring enough to provide for needs (or, at least, treats!) In regard to its Latin root, surely milk and cookies would help in relating to a stranger or enemy! The Bible has something to say about this in Hebrews 10:20: "If your enemy is hungry, feed him; if he is thirsty, give him something to drink." A woman I know took a homemade apple pie to someone she felt had become her enemy over a disagreement. That step of hospitality began the process toward a healed relationship.

The focus of true hospitality is the guest, and the emphasis is how you can best go about taking care of that guest. Let's look at a simple definition of hospitality:

"Given to generous and cordial welcome of guests, offering a pleasant or sustaining environment."

Milk and cookies fits right in there!

My brother Steve is a pastor, and he is continually opening his home to people. Once he mentioned to me, "I've learned that I can always offer somebody a glass of water, and often that's all the person really wants or needs."

I've tried to practice this great idea. It's simple, I have water on hand, and it helps me keep focused on what hospitality really is—serving my guest.

I read once: "When someone steps into our home, we make ourselves in charge of their happiness." Well, of course, we're not responsible for everyone's happiness, but that mindset is a good one, don't you think? We need to ask: What would make this guest feel honored? What would be most comfortable? What would make this guest feel satisfied? How can I show that I care?

And because we show we care, others will understand that God cares.

Not only is hospitality practical service for others, but it also reflects God's heart. If one is truly hospitable, one shows graciousness, courtesy, and genuine kindness—all qualities of our loving God. Someone can show these qualities without owning table settings for twelve with matching linen napkins.

My friend Donna told me that the hardest part of hospitality is trying too hard to impress with appearance and presentation instead of being genuinely warm and welcoming. Emphasizing these things can leave her feeling superficial and flat rather than warm, loving and satisfied. She said, "I have to remind myself that entertaining is not the same thing as hospitality. I need to slow down and take time to nurture relationships."

She's right. I need to remind myself of the same thing, especially when I end up running around at the last minute, barking orders at the family to help me finish whatever isn't, and making a general mess of a kind and loving atmosphere all in the name of "making things nice for the company."

True hospitality is "relationship-based" rather than "show-off based." When our goal is to impress someone with our home decor or cooking skills, we are more concerned with showing off rather than the wonderful potential of developing a relationship over that simple cup of tea or glass of water.

Kristen, thirty-two, and returning to college to finish her degree, didn't quite fit into the college group scene. I asked her for lunch, and we ended up sitting in the guest bedroom with soup bowls on our laps. This was during the part of our house remodel when the front walls and windows were missing, and it was too cold at the dining table. The space heater in the bedroom helped immensely, and Kristen didn't care where we sat or what we ate. She just needed a friend to get her started in this new phase of her life, and I was glad to extend a first step of friendship.

Whether you open a can of soup on the spur of the moment or spend all afternoon in the kitchen preparing a gourmet meal, welcoming a guest with a warm and loving spirit begins the relationship. I was reminded once again while sitting down with a new friend amidst the upheaval of a home construction (destruction?) project that it's the heart that matters, not the house.

Karen Mains states it so well from her classic book *Open Heart, Open Home*:

"True hospitality comes before pride. It has nothing to do with impressing people, but everything to do with making them feel welcome and wanted."

## Breaking the Pattern

Hospitality can seem difficult because we have the wrong idea of what it's supposed to be, or we've never seen it up-close the way God intended. I interviewed my mom about hospitality because I thought she was a pro; but after a few questions, I found out that she definitely hadn't started out that way.

She told me that her mother had never entertained, so she didn't have any idea of how to go about it. When she was first married, Mom was scared to death to have anyone over to the house.

Early in their marriage, my dad invited the deacon board over for pie and coffee. Now, Mom could make a great pie, but she didn't know how to make coffee. After placing the pie slices on each plate, and then scoops of ice cream by each, she discovered that she couldn't take the vacuum seal off the top of the coffee pot. It was some new-fangled thing in the 1940s. She waited thirty minutes for the pot to cool off so she could remove it. By then the ice cream had completely melted, and she was, in her words, "totally mortified."

I said, "Mom, why didn't you just serve the pie early and tell them the coffee was the real dessert? Half the men were engineers; they probably would've jumped at the chance to get at that coffee pot." She said she would do that now, but at that time, she felt far too insecure and embarrassed.

By the time I came along—number four—hosting company at our house was a weekly experience. But Mom hadn't started out that way. Her open hospitality developed over time and practice. At my folks' fiftieth anniversary party, friend after friend stood up to say they had first met my parents at church and then were promptly invited over for sandwiches and soup after the evening service.

Here's the point: My mom overcame her upbringing and insecurity, and she did it through years of practice. She and my Aunt Joy would have each other's family over every other Sunday—pot roast at my aunt's and roast chicken at our house (all on time-bake, of course)—partly, my mom said, so that they could practice having company. After all, it is referred to as "practicing hospitality," and practice is easier alongside those with whom we're comfortable.

My mom broke the pattern of the hospitality insecurity she had learned in her home of origin and started a new one in our family—one that my brothers and sisters have continued to pass down. It always amazes me to find out just how many people are at my sisters' homes for Thanksgiving or Easter, or how many roasts and turkeys were consumed and how many extra ovens were needed. And we all know how to make coffee.

Perhaps you did not grow up in a hospitable home but you forged ahead anyway. It took courage; you relied on God for strength, because you saw the value of changing the cycle of fear or pride.

If you haven't yet broken the cycle, you can start today.

--It's worth the risk and effort for your own sake as well as for others. I've done it, because I was desperate for friends; if they didn't invite me, I would invite them.

--It's worth whatever it takes for your kids' sake—so they won't have to go through the same insecurities you've experienced.

--It's worth the courage and time it takes for all of those who need your invitation and welcome. So many magazine articles refer to the isolation and depression that people experience today. Americans are proud of their independence; but the flipside of that self-reliance is isolation and loneliness.

COME TO MY TABLE

--It's worth the work and time, because an open home reflects God's open heart. People need to be invited and welcomed so they can know that God welcomes them. You be the one to do the inviting, with no thought to the condition of your couch or your pie-making ability!

~~

# Easy-As-Pie Vinegar Pie Crust

(Truly easy—I would never make a pie or quiche if my sister-in-law, Karen hadn't given me this recipe. It makes at least 4 pie crusts; I keep extras in the freezer.)

Break 1 egg into a glass measuring cup, add water until ¾ full. Add 1 T. vinegar and 1 t. baking powder, stir. It will foam. In a large bowl, mix 4 cups flour, 2 t. salt, and 4 t. sugar. Cut in 2 cups solid shortening. Add liquid and combine. Divide into 4 or 5 balls and freeze separately in wax paper, or roll out and use immediately.

# Chapter 2

# True Hospitality—How to Get Started

For a few months awhile back, my parents had a policewoman sleeping in the guest room. Lt. Rebecca Brown stopped my then eighty-eight-year-old dad for speeding. During the genial conversation that ensued, she mentioned that she could use a place to stay a couple nights a week while on duty in their town, so they offered the front bedroom and the little bathroom shower. She stashed her sleeping bag and pillow there, so it was no extra work for Mom, and they felt pretty special (and safe) with their own private officer at hand. Dad didn't get a ticket, either.

People who heard of Hyatt and Betty Moore's unusual houseguest just smile and say it sounds like them. And Mom and Dad took every opportunity to share the Lord with their new friend.

What makes one person love hospitality and the other run from it? Background and temperament do have much to do with it. However, if my mom hadn't worked through the lack of hospitality in her own upbringing, Lt. Rebecca Brown would still be traveling two hours to work each way several days a week.

Some might argue, why not just leave hosting for the extroverts and the good cooks? If you aren't comfortable having someone over, is it really necessary to make any changes? Isn't it just too much effort?

It sure can be, but Lt. Brown is glad my mom made the effort and broke out of her childhood pattern. And Mom would be the first to tell you the great joy she receives from her open door policy.

### Three Good Reasons to Be Hospitable

Hospitality isn't always easy, but we can be motivated and excited to do it because of three reasons:

- When we are hospitable, we give God joy.
- When we are hospitable, we show God's heart to others.
- When we are hospitable, we train our families to be God's welcome in this world.

~~~

First, we give God joy when we obey Him, and we obey when we are hospitable. We might have the impression that only some people have a special gift of hospitality, so they are the only ones who really need to exercise it. But the Bible calls everyone to this extraordinary opportunity.

In the midst of reminding us to do God's will and love each other with enthusiasm, the Bible states, "Be hospitable to one another without complaint" (1 Peter 4: 9). In Hebrews 13:2, we're told, "Don't forget to be hospitable to strangers . . ."

The writers assume that we know what they're talking about, because we're given no details. They just make sure we know that we have to do it. No mention of etiquette rules or a particular menu.

I think that means the type of hospitality we practice must not be of much concern to God. Whether we invite a crowd or one person; whether we serve hot dogs or roast beef isn't an issue for Him. The important issue is the doing of it. And in doing, we show love for friends and strangers.

The bottom line is this: give of yourselves, your homes, your provisions and your time. If there is a need, provide for it; and while you're at it, don't complain about it.

God understands that hospitality can be a challenge, because He included that little injunction "without complaint." Your darling husband may call at 4:30 in the afternoon (Oh, yes, that was *my* darling husband), and say, "Do you have extra for dinner tonight, honey?"

Will your answer be, "Of course, dear, how many were you thinking of inviting?" or "Are you kidding? We can't have company! The house is a mess and it's Monday, so we're only having spaghetti, and besides, I'm tired!" Not complaining while being hospitable is part of the obedience. That makes sense, doesn't it? If I hosted with a rotten attitude, I can't see how I would be pleasing God very much. Your guests might never know, but He does, and we do it first and foremost to please Him. An attitude adjustment can be more challenging than menu planning, but God is an expert in both, and He is always ready to help when we ask.

We delight Him by hosting others because He told us that when we offer a drink to someone else for His sake, it's as if we've offered it to Jesus Himself.

Every Sunday, twelve-year-old Shelby elbows her mom in church and asks, "Who can we have for dinner today?" Shelby is initiating goodness and charity to the Lord Himself. These are acts of mercy and kindness that any ordinary person can do every day. They do not depend on wealth, ability or intelligence. They are simple acts of inviting and serving that are freely given and freely received. And when we do them for others, we do them for Jesus. Of course He is delighted!

In Matthew, Jesus said, "For I was hungry, and you gave Me something to eat; I was thirsty, and you gave Me something to drink; I was a stranger, and you invited Me in . . . to the extent that you did it to one of these brothers of Mine, even the least of them, you did it to Me" (Matthew 25:35 40).

He said, "When you helped others, you helped Me."

Now that's a motivation that can keep me going through all the extra laundry and dishes! We have a chance to serve the Son of God at our table and offer Him a cup and plate filled to the brim whenever we give the same to our guest.

~~~

A second reason to be hospitable is the great fun and privilege we have to show others what God's heart is like. When it comes to hospitality, it's easy to answer the question, "WWJD?" This is what Jesus would do:

He would step out on the porch and call out names until he had a block party. Or, He would quietly ask His neighbor in for tea and cookies from Trader Joe's.

God put out the first welcome mat at creation, and He continued to invite mankind to Himself through the work of redemption. He's our best example. When we do the welcoming and the inviting, we are the hands and feet of Jesus to our world. Adding an extra hamburger to the grill so one more can come to the table is an ordinary act for an extraordinary purpose.

Hosting and inviting and welcoming are part of Jesus' nature. So, to be more like Him, we host and invite and welcome. We do it imperfectly because we're not quite as good as He is; we make mistakes but we go ahead and try because we want to be like Him.

When Jan met Mila, she thought Mila might need a friend, so she invited her over for coffee. They spoke about their kids, the local school system, their lives before becoming mothers. Jan invited Mila to hear her speak at her ladies' church group, and Mila came. They continued to see each other off and on.

It was two years later when Mila called Jan in a panic. "Jan, are you busy? Can I come over? I'd like to talk about spiritual things." That day, Jan introduced Mila to a personal relationship with Christ. It all started with an invitation to coffee. Mila knew that when she needed help, she could go to someone—Jan—who knew God.

People may not come to know God unless they feel His welcome through a person. That person might be you. Somewhere along the way, someone may have gotten the message that Christ is unapproachable—He's too big, too vague, too harsh, too impersonal. But when you open your front door and say, "Come on in!" you show your guest that God has welcomed her as well.

God says, "Come on over, I've set a place for you, and there's one for your friend. Why don't you ask him, too?" And so we do, because it's just what He would do.

Maybe you have already taken God up on His invitation and given Him your heart. But what about the world waiting for you at home or in your neighborhood or in your extended family circle or at work? What about the person God has placed in your life that doesn't yet have a clue that she has a place card with her name etched in gold (or Crayola) at His table? God's welcome is the world's welcome, and it can come through you.

Jesus said, "I've made you light, so let your light shine, keep open house, be generous with your lives. By opening up to others, you'll prompt people to open up with God, this generous Father in heaven" (Matthew 5:14-16, *THE MESSAGE*). Do our lives reflect God's generosity? They can, simply by using the time-honored words: "Want to come over for a bite to eat?"

~~~

The third reason to be hospitable is so we can train our children to be God's heart to others. My friend Bonnie is fond of saying, "More is caught than taught." When our kids see us keep an open house and being generous with our lives, they learn how to be God's light. This training can be fun, and it will translate into an ease of hosting and welcoming that will become as natural to them as breathing when they grow up.

Debbi is not comfortable with hospitality. Yet, she wants to be obedient to God and desires that her kids become hospitable people. So she has decided to host people in their home every Sunday night. Right now, the regular guests are a young married couple who need to spend time with a family and feel at home in Deb's house. They come each time, and lately Deb has included another friend or two to round out the table and bring refreshment to their souls.

Now, this looks like a simple action, and it is. But the ramifications are huge! These friends, and sometimes strangers, get to eat a family meal together once a week. They prepare food together and share stories about the week's happenings. Maybe best of all, Debbi's two teenagers are taking it all in, becoming friends with adults other than their parents, seeing the Christian life lived out through the lively discussions around the table, and working together to make it happen (and clean it up.) When they get older, Seth and Rebekkah will see their homes as not only private places in which to live and grow, but also as open houses to include the people God brings into their lives for His sake and for His kingdom.

Our kids are quick learners, and it's always great to teach little ones some doorway etiquette. Simple niceties such as, "Welcome! Come on in, I'll get my mom. Can I take your coat?" can be practiced with role-play and learned quickly. I'm sure your friends would be impressed with such treatment, but that's not the reason behind the training. Rather, the idea is to teach our children the preciousness of people, and that when they are kindly polite to a friend or a stranger, they honor God.

Children easily understand that if they do something kind for someone, it's a way of showing love for Jesus. As your kids see you make banana bread for a sick friend or invite a new neighbor for coffee, they will grow up knowing the value and ease of spreading a little joy with a simple act of kindness. (And take them with you when you drop off that banana bread.)

When I was growing up, our home was the gathering place for the church youth group parties, adult Sunday School parties and Good News Clubs. I took it for granted that a home is to be used—the more company, the better. Of course, the carpet got worn and dishes broken. One year, the shower door cracked from top to bottom from a great game of sardines—too many teenagers packed into a small space! The house was never picture perfect, but we were comfortable inviting our friends over, and they liked to come.

Open House on Christmas night was an annual event, and we kids were delighted to welcome the Millers and the Elliotts each year, as well as any newcomers. The tradition was a rich one, to be continued in the Donaldson family—maybe a little differently, but carried on nonetheless. When someone asks me why it's not a problem to have people over for coffee, I say, "It's because my mother did." What a gift you will give your children if someday they can say the same of you!

~~~

The more we understand that we are doing hospitality for God, the deeper our motivation will run. And the more we practice hospitality, the easier it becomes and the more joy we will give God, ourselves and others.

~~~

# Four Steps to Getting Started

No matter how much you love God, you still may feel stuck and insecure when it comes to opening your home to people. If I had to face all of my fears in one day, I would never have anyone over. So here are four tips that will help you get started.

## Start Small

Invite just one person—a single person needs an invitation, and he or she doesn't eat as much as a whole family. A college student needs a family away from home. He or she may eat as much as a whole family but is always so grateful for anything you serve! Invite your child's teacher for tea after school—your child will learn how to serve and will love the special attention. If you invite a family, it's simpler to order a pizza than plan a gourmet meal. I was the guest at such a meal, and we enjoyed the time just as much on the floor around the coffee table than at a formal table. Invite a family for dessert—not a whole dinner-—it saves time and money and can accomplish the same end. Plan your hospitality on a smaller scale, if that makes it easier for you, and the more you practice the more confident you will become.

## Start Simple

Serve tea or lemonade and Pepperidge Farm cookies. I keep chocolate mints in my freezer and serve them on the teacup saucer if someone stops by—they defrost by the time the water boils, and a little chocolate helps make a friend. Look for a yummy recipe that uses ingredients that have a good shelf life. It's simple to whip up something for last-minute company if you already have everything on hand (see pantry list ideas in chapter 8). Find what's easiest for you, and do it more than once. No one will know you served it to your last set of company; and with less preparation to worry about, you can more easily keep your mind on your guests and their needs. My friend keeps a popcorn basket on her coffee table. If someone drops in, the basket is quickly filled and everyone gathers round. Popcorn is inexpensive, easy to fix and a welcome treat.

Nowhere does the Bible command us to throw elaborate dinner parties in a perfectly cleaned home. What the Bible does say is that we are to offer whatever we have to God and to each other, no matter how small or how imperfect that may be.

If God has given you the ability and joy in providing elaborate dinner parties, then do them with His blessing and strength. If He's given you five kids and a small budget, do picnics at the park or take muffins and coffee to the school secretary. If you're single in a studio apartment, go ahead and have that potluck, or have everyone bring munchies that begin with their middle initial. Each situation can be as simple as you make it, and is a wonderful way to make a new friend(s) and be God's welcome to someone.

## Start by Using Your Own Style

You may not know what your style is until you start doing it. You don't need to mimic another person's style unless it's just a way to find out what you like doing best. You'll find out what your style is by practicing and trying new things. Some people love using good china, others prefer paper plates.

My friend Trish is a fabulous cook. She told me that's what she enjoys about hospitality—making everyone happy about what they're eating! She doesn't always get out the good dishes—

it can be Corelle or paper plates—but, believe me, we don't care when we're sinking our teeth into her cooking.

Your style may be to think about the décor or to concentrate on family activities. My kids enjoy hosting "s'mores" parties in our fireplace, especially if it's raining. It's messy but worth it. You may prefer a buffet on the counter or a blanket on the floor. My kitchen is small, but with large crowds, people can pick up a plate and make their way through one doorway and out another. When I'm being myself, I'm inviting my guests to be themselves as well. And when I'm comfortable with myself, I can concentrate more on the other person.

## Start with a Servant Heart

Hospitality is for the sake of the guest. We don't do it to make ourselves look good. As someone comes through the door, think: What would make this guest feel honored? Comfortable? Satisfied? How can I show him or her that I care? How can I be Jesus to this person? Jesus washed feet, fried fish on the beach, broke bread and blessed it, and gave His very life for others. That's servanthood.

Paul wrote in Philemon 7: "Your love has given me great joy and encouragement, because you, brother, have refreshed the hearts of the saints."

That's what is so much fun—to refresh another's heart whether or not the floor got vacuumed or the meal was perfect. I've noticed that the ones who seem to need refreshment the most are working moms, so I invited some of my neighbors for a Saturday breakfast. I wanted them to feel pampered and refreshed, even for just a couple of hours. Being a servant is part of hospitality because it involves work on our part. But it's worth the time and effort because we know that we can surround others with His love and peace and soul-refreshment.

We serve another because he or she needs it, and God has brought this person our way for His purpose.

Ask God to help you get started. Keep it simple and small to begin with, and watch how He delights in using you to refresh someone's heart. And keep a lookout at garage sales for the perfect popcorn basket for your table. Here's a simple favorite; and remember, chocolate can help make a friend.

~~

# Marshmallow Chocolate Pie

Use one baked and cooled 9-inch pie shell. Melt together in saucepan:

27 marshmallows, ¾ cup milk. Whisk together one 6 oz. pkg. chocolate chips until melted. Cool completely. Fold mixture into one 12 oz. cool whip. Pour into pie shell. Chill for one hour or more. Sprinkle with nuts and serve with additional whipped cream. Yum!

# Chapter 3

# Hosting Like Him

Every Monday afternoon, women gather in Joanie's kitchen for chocolate. It's presented in various, luscious ways: cocoa, triple chocolate crock-pot cake, chocolate dipped biscotti, the list goes on and on. (If you're drooling, take heart. I've included some of their favorites in Chapter 8.) The ladies come, not just to get their chocolate quota for the week, but because they know they are welcome. They share their hearts. They know they will be listened to and leave encouraged. It's more than chocolate, much more. Joanie's kitchen is a workout place for the soul. Friends gather and gain strength for the week ahead . . . and maybe a new recipe or two.

I love the fact that a simple afternoon of chocolate and friends is a way of reflecting the heart of God. And God loves it, too.

Hospitality simply means making people comfortable and at home; and we want our guests to not only feel at home in our house, but to feel at home with God, and He with them. *"And I pray that Christ will be more and more at home in your hearts, living within you as you trust in Him"* (Ephesians 3:17 LB). It reminds me of the old *Beverly Hillbillies* song: "Take your shoes off, sit a spell." As we cultivate a home with Christ as the centerpiece, we can present God's inviting heart to others. And it becomes part of our identity as well.

J. I. Packer wrote, in his classic book *Knowing God*, "Loving one another is the family likeness of God's children." Opening our homes is a way to love, and it shows off the family resemblance. We invite others because God invited us to begin with. He is our example, our inspiration and the motivation that keeps us at it when we have to run to the store for more milk or change the bed sheets one more time. Hospitality is not about how and what, it's about who. God loving people is the main point.

When we know the Ultimate Host, we can learn to host like Him. We can create an atmosphere and environment that welcomes our guests not only to our table, but to His.

## Creating the Welcome -- What's in the Air?

The principles of the Chinese practice of *feng shui*, as applied to home decorating, hit America by storm. Creating balance and serenity is what counts. According to this philosophy, our decorating choices can alter our relationships, efficiency, health and prosperity. From what I've read about it, my home is not even close to presenting such a tranquil setting in line with its design standards. If I decide it's the way to go, it may just be too hard to give away all my favorite garage sale finds!

*Feng shui* aside, God does want our homes to promote peace, and He will help us craft an atmosphere that embraces our guests with His welcome and tranquility. His perfect balance includes warmth and joy, as well as a whole lot of love and fun kicked in, and it doesn't necessarily have to do with where we place the couch, the houseplants and the indoor water fountains. (The fun part comes when we remember to put food coloring in the water fountain—green for St. Patrick's Day and red for Valentine's!)

One way to help you host like Him is to answer these questions:

• What are the ingredients for making me feel welcome in another person's home?

• What has made me feel special when I've been formally invited to a special event or I've just dropped in on a close friend?

Here are some "welcoming ingredients" that come to my mind:

~A genuine, warm greeting at the door: "So glad you're here! It's great you were able to come. Let me take your coat."

~Networking introductions between guests: "Mom, this is Debbi. She's organized, like you— she alphabetized all my spices!"

~The host who stops what she's doing to give attention to her guest or includes her guest in the meal preparation: "Would you like to join me in the kitchen? I'm not quite ready to put the food on."

~The fragrance of the meal cooking or potpourri simmering: A cinnamon stick in a saucepan of boiling water isn't fancy, but it warmly seasons the atmosphere.

~A fire burning in the fireplace: This is especially good on a rainy day. No wood or no fireplace? No problem—light a candle or two for your table. Even for a morning coffee, candlelight is pretty and simple.

~Put on the teakettle or start the coffee: Both can be done while you're still welcoming an unexpected guest. To make it special, add a few drops of vanilla to your coffee before perking— it adds a subtle flavor and fragrance.

~Ask questions (and listen to the answers): "How was the traffic? Did you have a good day? Was it difficult finding our place?"

~Warm and comfortable furnishings: An elderly guest may prefer a hardbacked chair over a softer one. Pull dining chairs into the living room for extra seating if needed, and offer pillows or afghans to make guests feel cozy.

These are only a few welcoming ideas. Perhaps you thought of other "feel welcome" ingredients.

The point is this: *Do any of us need more money or a bigger house or a witty personality to do any of the above?* I don't think so. We just need to extend the invitation in the first place and put on an extra plate.

When a new family came to our door one evening for dinner, the meal wasn't quite ready, and they were on time. But Mark had the fire going and the girls (plus Sunny, the dog) flocked to the entryway to bid them enter. First impressions are important, and what my new friend said later was, "What a welcome we felt—the fire was going, you were cutting bread at the breadboard, we almost tripped over the dog, but we felt like you wanted us there."

God wanted them there, too. We host like Him by letting others know the same. "You're welcome here because God brought you here; why don't you come into the kitchen and help me get the food on the table? Oh, and watch out for the dog!"

There is no one more hospitable than God. He chose us and invited us so that we could pass on the invitation to others.

*"Blessed is the man whom You choose and cause to approach You, that he may dwell in Your courts"* (Psalm 65:4).

Acceptance is a main ingredient in hosting people like God

does. But they may not come to know God unless they feel the welcome of a person. That person might be you. Somewhere along the way, someone may have gotten the message that Christ is unapproachable—He's too big, too vague, too harsh, too impersonal. But when you open your front door and say, "Come on in!" you show your guests that God has welcomed them as well.

In church one Sunday, Lynn sat behind a couple that made her feel uncomfortable. They kept acting like newlyweds. It looked like a second marriage. (It was!) During church, she kept thinking about different people who would be good to counsel them to be a little more restrained in public. She finally came to the conclusion that they just needed to feel accepted and have more friends. So she invited them for dinner for the following Sunday. Later that week, Lynn said she panicked: "Why did I invite them? They probably won't enjoy it. They might not like our family." But, they *did* like them, they were very easy to talk to, the guests enjoyed the simple food and asked for all the recipes! She added, "It turned out to be so worthwhile, and here I was thinking all through church that morning, 'Oh, well, it can only be a few hours for us to put up with each other!'"

God had something else in mind, in spite of Lynn's initial impressions and bits of panic. She invited them in and turned strangers into friends. That's what God did for you and me.

Once we were strangers, but now through Christ, we have become His friends.

*"But now in Christ Jesus you who once were far away have been brought near through the blood of Christ"* (Ephesians 2:12). He took the first step, like Lynn, and instead of judging, invited us in.

At a very formal dinner party, all the guests were dressed in tuxes and formal attire—all except for one man who wore a simple sports coat and no tie. At the head of the table, the elegant host glanced over the company, quietly noting the man who didn't quite fit in. Without comment, he got up from his chair, removed his tux jacket, placed it over the back of the chair, loosened his tie and removed it, and then sat back down. The rest of the guests, not to be outdone (or overdressed), quickly followed his example, and soon everyone was equally casual.

Here was a host who, above all, wanted his guest to feel accepted and at home. Rather than make even one guest feel out of place, he placed his rightful elegance aside for the comfort of another. He didn't care to impress, but simply to care.

God the Father took off the formal coat of His majesty by becoming a man, the Son, Jesus. *". . . Jesus didn't cling to His rights as God, but laid aside His mighty power and glory, taking the disguise of a slave, and becoming like men" (Philippians 2:5-7).* We are accepted in Him. And because we are, we can accept and invite one another into our homes and hearts.

We can welcome others because we are assured of God's welcome to us. Charles Spurgeon's daily devotional, *Morning and Evening,* tells us (April 12):

"We are invited to come as we are—in distress, in fear, in depression, in a feeling of separateness from God. We can come because Christ has been here before us."

Those who come to our door may be in distress or fear or depression, or they may just need a friend. They can come to God, find all the tranquility they will ever need all because you show that they are welcome, too.

## Who's on the Guest List—Creating the Opportunity

I once was a guest in a home where the breadboard in the kitchen was pulled out with a tea service on it. I asked my hostess, "What is this for?" She replied, "It's for any guest who may come by." She wasn't expecting anyone in particular. No formal invitations had been sent. She was ready to serve, expectantly waiting to wait on others and maybe meet a need or two. And she did it with style and beauty.

We don't have to pull out our breadboard (I would never be able to open the dishwasher if I did), but we can have the same attitude of expectancy and anticipation. What an exciting way to look at our day: *I wonder whom God will bring across my path today?* Each new person may be one who may not have met the Ultimate Friend, Jesus, and we can be that connection—we can be the one who makes the introductions.

Right now you may be thinking, *Whom should I invite? Is there anyone out there who would really enjoy coming to my house? People don't just drop in as much anymore. They always seem to be too busy, or think that I might be.*

God's guest list includes the world, so to host like Him, you can put everyone on your list that He's placed in your world. That could be your child's teacher, the school secretary, your Clinique salesclerk, your next-door neighbor (or next to the next-door neighbor), the soccer coach, other soccer parents, a favorite waitress, your dentist's receptionist, a visiting missionary, your in-laws—the list is as long as the people you meet.

We live in a college town, and I'm always amazed at the number of people living here who are from other countries. I've met many women, whose husbands teach at the university, who are from Jordan, Egypt, Iran, and Pakistan. They need tea and friends because they are in a strange place a long way from home.

They are delighted to come and delightful to know. My sister met several such women when her husband attended graduate school. These other young wives loved coming to Lori's humble apartment and spending time together. They even asked her to teach them how to make fresh strawberry pie, and she did. Lori took the opportunity to invite from God's list—the world—and she didn't even have to leave her neighborhood.

Rather than a mindset of *Does God want me to have someone over?* try on this new way of thinking: *God, who do You want me to invite?* Not "if," but "who." Ask Him for His list and make it yours.

Ask the Lord: "Is there someone You have in mind that I can invite for Your sake and with Your blessing (and help)?"

He knows your day, your week, your month. He knows your capacity and strength and what's in the cupboard. You can give Him your schedule, and something more—a heart of expectancy. He will work out the details, while delighting in your heart that looks a little bit more like His. Whomever God places in your path on any given day is to be invited to Jesus. And it can begin with an invitation to your table.

The Bible says it this way: "And God has given us the privilege of urging everyone to come into His favor and be reconciled to Him . . . as though God were entreating through us, receive the love He offers you" (2 Corinthians 5:18,20, *TLB*).

One Sunday morning, my friend Ces was seated behind four college students. She put that entreaty into practice and invited them for chili and cornbread after church. They loved it, and so did her family.

Our hospitality is God's entreaty to the world. Does your home and hearth entreat others to the One who loves them most?

We all have built-in relationships: students, colleagues, clerks, neighbors. But the built-in relationship that is most common, that we can sometimes forget, is family—both immediate and extended.

First Peter 4: 9 says, "Be hospitable to one another without complaint." Sometimes the "one anothers" closest to us cause the most complaining in us! We can forget that our own children and husbands need our best welcome.

I heard storyteller and radio personality Garrison Keillor say, on his *Prairie Home Companion* broadcast: "Children can always smell hospitality. They know if they are welcome. To make people feel welcome is pure art. By practicing it you discover things you wouldn't otherwise know."

Welcoming your family first means a smile, then it means including them in the planning and preparation (and cleanup). It means that you make things special just for them, not just for company.

Last night, I finally put out the beautiful white twisted tapers that had been a gift many years before. I had been saving them for something special. When they saw the candles, the girls asked, "Who's coming for dinner?" I said, "No one . . . it's just for you." The candles were somewhat dusty—I had waited a little too long. But I realized I needed to make my family feel God's grand welcome. What better way than setting a nice table with a good meal and just us as the guests? And what better way for them to learn how to offer that same welcome to their friends?

Jesus showed us that children were important to Him when He invited them up on His lap (see Mark 10:14). That was an invitation that even surprised His followers. Do our kids feel Jesus' welcome in their own homes?

I remember going to Julie's house when I was growing up. None of us kids were allowed to walk through the living room, even the kids who lived there. I wondered who did go in . . .

only the adults, I imagined, but I rarely saw anyone there. Many years later, the day we got our new couch, I felt tempted to do as Julie's mom did. "The couch is off-limits!" I wanted to say. It looked so beautiful that first week, but I knew it wasn't realistic to place a "keep off" sign in front of it. Things are meant to be used, and people are meant to be loved—not the other way around. When our things become more important than people, our kids will easily pick up on what we value most.

You can begin a warm in-house welcome tonight with a candlelight dinner just because, or a picnic on the floor, if that's your style. No special reason other than it's your family that's special. At the same time, it's always good to teach the kids to say after every meal, "Thank you for the good dinner." (Maybe in our kids' minds it was only a good meal for our dog, Sunny, but it's still good training!) I love the mother who taught her children to *"rise up and call her 'blessed'"* after every meal, as it says in Proverbs 31:28. And they will feel blessed, in turn, by your special welcome.

Do our kids feel the freedom to invite their friends in? I was a little startled when I went over to Diane's house for the first time and saw a full-sized Ping Pong table in her front room. When I commented on it, she just said, "We wanted our home to be where the kids wanted to gather with their friends. That way, we would know where they were!" A smart woman! She let her kids and their friends know that they were welcome in a very fun and practical way.

Not only can we see God's guest list including built-in relationships, but we can easily expand the list by taking advantage of built-in opportunities to get together. Such normal occasions include holiday gatherings, birthday celebrations, the play-offs of a favorite team or sport, welcoming the first day of spring, saying farewell to summer, sending a kid off to kindergarten or college, a job promotion, even a job loss. One year, we acknowledged a struggling economy with a Recession

Soup Night. (We made potluck "stone soup" and wore clothes that we had owned longer than five years.)

Showing God's hospitality begins with this idea: *Because God has welcomed me, I too, will welcome you. And if you come to know me, you'll begin to understand God's welcome.* God took the initiative by inviting you and me. We can do the same by creating the opportunity, making our guest list from those we know or want to know, and letting Him do the hosting through us.

One Sunday, Suzanne looked a little lost. Her best friend had moved away a month before, and in addition to that, this was the first week that her adopted family had not been at church—they, too, had made an out-of-state job change. Ellen, noticing her sad expression, wanted to do something about it. Despite the fact that her day was already full, she went over to Suzanne and said, "I know Gary and Robyn are gone. Would you like to come for lunch today? But [without missing a beat], is it okay if you stay just an hour? Because I'm stripping the wallpaper in our kitchen and need to get it done before this second baby comes."

Suzanne was glad to come over that day, and she stayed much longer than an hour, sharing her life story while helping Ellen strip wallpaper all afternoon. Since that time, Suzanne has helped Ellen's family with many home projects, including painting and wallpapering. And Suzanne joins them each Thanksgiving and Christmas, and has been officially adopted as "Aunt Suzanne" by [now] three little girls.

If you want to begin to host like Jesus, you and your family could choose one day a month or week to be "company day" and plan your grocery list around a meal that calls for a little more. Some people don't mind a spontaneous invitation. If you find that your stew could feed more than your family, call a new friend to join you that evening. Planned in advance or last-minute company doesn't matter to God. He just wants us to be ready and willing to pick up the phone and offer His welcome.

## What's On the Menu—Creating a Sustaining Environment

When Jesus prepared a meal on the beach one morning, He hosted one of the first potlucks (see John 21). His friends brought the entrée, and He provided the side dish. No mention of dessert or beverage, but everyone seemed satisfied, and a lot more went on than just what was eaten. Yet isn't that what we think about when we think of hospitality? Food! I might even call my friend and ask, "Do you have any chocolate?" If it's a yes, I'm right there. The four food groups wrapped up in one. Christ and His followers must have felt that two food groups were enough as they met around a beach fire early one morning after a long night of fishing.

Here we witness one of the most intimate conversations between Jesus and His friends, and it began with a simple invitation: "Come and have breakfast—bread and a fish fry." Following that simple meal, Jesus asked Peter three times: "Do you love Me?" Shortly before this, Peter had denied Christ three times. Now Peter had an opportunity to feel Christ's forgiveness as well as reveal his heart to his Lord. Peter's response was an impassioned, "Yes, Lord, You know I love You!" This was no light table talk.

Jesus continued, "If you love Me then show it by following Me and feeding My lambs. And ultimately you will die for Me" (see John 21:17-19).

This precious interchange between Peter and his Master is the most significant event of the passage, not what they had to eat. The menu, the number of courses, the preparation, the presentation—none of that mattered in light of the dialogue that followed. What a great example of the meal being the vehicle for something bigger! Food paved the way for encouragement and companionship and meaningful relationship to take place. "Come and have breakfast" was an invitation Jesus used to change a man's life. Once again we see God hosting through this simple statement: "Come and drink and eat. You'll feel better if you do. And then we'll get to what's really important. I'll teach you how to live, and even how to die."

God wants to use our hospitality as a means for Him to change lives—and the lives of those we invite—no matter what we serve on the table. Does it involve food? Usually. But food is not the main event.

One evening, seven of Janell's favorite friends came over for dinner. I was happy to be one of them. We had offered to bring something but were secretly glad she turned us down. Janell is a fabulous cook, and we knew we were in for a treat. It didn't matter what she served, it was sure to be delicious. As we arrived, mouthwatering fragrance greeted us from the kitchen. Soon we were enjoying succulent stuffed pork tenderloin with Marsala sauce, homemade rolls, mashed sweet potatoes, and fancy green beans. She told us she wanted to bless us. Her gift to her friends was a meal carefully planned, deliciously prepared and beautifully presented. We sighed blissfully with every bite.

Was the food the main event? You might think so. It certainly dominated much of the conversation. Yet, even with Janell's flair to please the palate with such ease and pleasure, the main event was not the menu. Rather, it was the heart behind the food. Janell wished to show us love. Our summer Bible study had just finished, and she had enjoyed it and us so much. She wanted to thank us in a way that she could—through her cooking. Expressing her appreciation to others through food is one way she blesses, and she does it effortlessly. She was as delighted as we were. As we savored each morsel, we knew she loved us. Love was the main course, not the tenderloin. God blessed us through Janell's cooking, and that is what mattered.

Does it matter what you cook? Or, that you can cook? Or, that you are a good cook? Sometimes. It does matter, a little. It's good to have something to serve your guests, be it a cookie or piece of cinnamon toast or a glass of iced tea. But what you need to remember is the word "little." Where we all get into trouble is when the food becomes all-consuming—no pun intended—so that we lose sleep nights wondering what to have, how we can afford it, where to buy it, how to prepare it, how much to prepare and when to get started. And maybe you've thought of a few more things to stew about (sorry, again, for the pun).

Stew, now that's a good thing to have. It's relatively inexpensive, it serves a lot, you can quickly add to it if you find your guest list is growing, and it makes the house smell wonderful. However, it's not great to serve it when it's 103 degrees outside and you've been working in the yard all day. In my early days of hosting, I was excited about being able to make chicken soup like my mother made, so I went ahead and made it and had Dave and Pat for a light supper after evening church. What I hadn't taken into account was the summer weather and our apartment's poor air conditioning. Our dear friends kindly sweated through a steaming bowl of homemade soup. Cold fruit soup or a turkey sandwich would have been a better choice. My mistake mattered, a little. Obviously, I've never forgotten it. I imagine they have.

God has not gifted all of us to cook like Janell. But He has made everyone with the capacity to love, and He wants us to create a sustaining environment whether or not that includes recipes from *Bon Appetit* or a cake mix from Betty Crocker. God will help you with the details—like weather and recipes. And to Him, food is just the details. The menu is used to accompany His plan, a plan of love and welcome and blessing.

If I thought I needed to host just like Joanie or Janell, I might start getting nervous. I don't cook with their panache. I'm sure they grate their parmesan, I'm just happy to find the green can in the refrigerator. I can't fit in an afternoon of friends on the same day every week, like Joanie does. I'm not sure how Janell makes her Marsala sauce. I'm not . . . I'm not . . . and the list could go on and on, if I let it. The important thing is to have the same love for God and people. It just comes out looking (and maybe, tasting) differently, and that's okay.

My friend DeDe grew up with a mother who made salad in a wading pool. Once a year the whole church came over for their annual "Hoe Down." The only thing big enough for a giant green salad was a child-sized blue plastic wading pool. I'm not sure what she tossed it with, but I know that they never forgot it. (DeDe did say her mom bought a new one each year.) The food and the bowl didn't matter. The fact that everyone could gather in one place once a year to eat together was the main event.

The good news is that God isn't interested in how your hospitality compares to another's. He just wants us to open our homes, put on an extra plate or two, and make the introductions. Hosting like Him means creating an environment of warmth, acceptance, and welcome.

Come to my table, you'll meet Jesus there, get a cup of soup or a pool-sized salad, and maybe play a game or two.

~~

# Four-Bean Chili for a Crowd

4 cans of beans of your choice, with liquid

3 cans diced tomatoes, with liquid, (Mexican style, optional)

1 ½ cups shredded cooked chicken, pork or beef

1 t. ground cumin

1 bay leaf

½ t. hot pepper sauce (optional)

Heat all ingredients in 4-qt. stockpot over med-high heat. Cook, stirring until it comes to a boil, reduce to low and cover. Simmer until it thickens, 25-30 minutes, stirring occasionally. Remove bay leaf. Serve with cornbread and tortilla chips.

# The Favor of a Reply Is Requested

## The Invitation

*"Get away with Me and you'll recover your life. I'll show you how to take a real rest. Walk with Me and work with Me, watch how I do it. Learn the unforced rhythms of grace."* (Matthew 11:28, *THE MESSAGE*).

"Now that you know Me, why don't you allow your life and home to invite another to know Me? I'll show you how. Don't sweat the small stuff. I'll take care of the details like who and what and where. You decide the when, and it will be great fun. Will you come and work with Me?"

## The RSVP

Lord,

What a great idea to be Your welcome! I have to tell You, though, my house isn't very big, I'm not the best cook, and right now the budget is already stretched to the limit. On the other hand, You did say You'd be with me . . . and I met the nicest person the other day. I bet she wouldn't mind store-bought cookies. And our kids could play while we get acquainted. Okay, I'll try it. Thanks for the idea, and I'm glad I won't have to do it alone. I'm wondering who else You might add to my guest list, maybe even tomorrow.

Now write your RSVP:

# Part II

# God's Hospitality

## *Prologue*

Hospitality began with God.

He stood at the edge of time, cupped His hands, and called out so that all would hear:

"Come on in!

"You're welcome here.

"Yes, here . . . right by Me, at My table.

"Come! Everyone's invited!"

Did you hear?

He means you, and the one next to you, too.

God is the consummate welcomer. He opens wide His door, welcomes us to His table, and serves a generous feast.

We who RSVP find that we have come home.

Once we are settling in to enjoy His company, we notice the

door is left slightly ajar. Curious, we push it open and step out onto the porch and hail our neighborhood:

"Come on in! You're welcome, too."

"Don't worry. We'll make room."

"The world was invited, after all, so please, please, come in."

Why be hospitable? Because God welcomed us first.

# Chapter 4

# God's Welcome

### Love at First Sight

A true welcome begins in the heart.

I remember the day daughter number three decided to arrive. Years before, we had accustomed our lives to a family of four. Two kids were good. Two were plenty of work, time, money and energy. We were content. Then came the surprise.

We were going to be more than four.

Friends would ask, "Are you surprised?"

"More like shock," I'd say.

In the ensuing months, we adjusted—our home, our furniture, our mindset, our hearts. Shock moved toward anticipation. We were getting a surprise treat from God.

In the beginning, we thought two. But He wanted three, and now we did too.

The day came at last. Phone calls were made, friends and family arrived. We waited and prepared and walked and prayed . . . and waited some more. Anticipation and hovering began in earnest.

Finally, she was ready. I cried, the doctor said "Push," and Mary Grace slipped into her new world, crying and wrinkled, red and gorgeous.

Love at first sight all around.

We had waited, adjusted, and eagerly prepared. We had even hovered the last twelve hours. And here she was.

"Little Mary Grace. You're so very welcome here. We love you, we wanted you, we waited for you, and you're finally here. Welcome."

~~

In the beginning, God created the heavens and the earth, and His Spirit hovered over the waters—waiting, guarding, protecting, anticipating . . . us.

In the beginning, God wanted us. He created the world. He hovered, He waited until the sixth day, and He created us. We were no surprise to Him.

First, He got the world ready, and then He invited us to join Him. God pursued us.

It wasn't our idea, it was God's. He was the original Host. He wanted us, so He sent out an invitation framed by stars and galaxies that could have read:

"You're welcome here. I made this world for you. Welcome to My world, to My life, to My heart. You won't need another thing. Please make yourself comfortable."

How do we know that God has a welcoming heart? And how can we be sure that we are included in His welcome?

We know because He told us, and He showed us. He was there first, and He invited us to join Him. And He showed us His welcome heart from the very beginning.

Genesis 1:1 reads: "In the beginning, God created the heavens and the earth."

"In the beginning." He acted first. He didn't have to. He didn't need us. He was fine as He was. But He went ahead and created our world.

Don't you feel it's nicer when someone else takes the initiative? When someone wants you and does something about it and invites you into their lives? That's what God did.

## God's Welcome vs. Our Welcome

What kind of welcome does God offer? Is it anything like the kind we provide?

Before I was married, I went with a friend to his home to visit his folks for the first time. I don't remember many of the details, except there seemed to be a definite chill in the air, and it was coming from my friend's mother. You see, I was dating her firstborn, and even though we were both adults, she did not seem to "approve" of me for her son.

Because she was a godly woman, she tried hard not to let it show, but I could tell. I did not feel welcome, and it was a bit hard to take. It took several years for us to accept each other.

I have to admit that I would have been more accepting of her if she had accepted me first. She was the host; I was the guest.

I was the intrusion. (Eventually, I felt her warm and loving heart. She welcomed me. In fact, she even came to my wedding. Maybe she was just happy it wasn't also her son's wedding!)

~~

A while ago, I called a friend who had moved out of the area and asked if she'd like to come to tea the next time she was in town. We scheduled a day and time.

A week or so later, I was working hard on clearing clutter in the closets when the doorbell rang. I was so irritated at being interrupted. I felt especially noble in working on de-cluttering, so I was all the more upset. I remember bursting out loud with something like: "Don't people know how busy I am? How am I ever going to get this job done?!"

I went to the door and there stood my friend with her three children. I graciously invited them in, put the teakettle on, and we had a good visit.

She never suspected that I had completely forgotten that she was coming, or that I had felt so annoyed at being interrupted.

~~

Another time, when I was experiencing some temporary brain loss, a missionary friend came to the door. Eyes wide, I recovered with what I thought was adequate enthusiasm:

"Great to see you, Donna!"

"You forgot I was coming, didn't you?" she responded.

Well, yes, I had, but of course it was still great to see her and to have her spend the night. . .

These three encounters are in direct contrast to God's welcome.

- Our Heavenly Father never gives us the cold shoulder.
- There is never a chill in the air when we step into His presence.
- He doesn't have to put on a good appearance or feign His love.
- We don't ever catch Him by surprise.
- God doesn't grumble all the way to the door.
- He is not a reluctant Host, irritated by the interruptions of His children.
- And, He never forgets that we are invited.

God took the initiative. He prepared the place. He sent out our invitation long ago, and He has a perfect memory.

## He Loved First

How do we know that God has a welcoming heart? And, how can we be sure that we are included in His welcome?

"We love, because He first loved us" (1 John 4:19).

Another "first." He loved us first. He spread out the welcome mat with love written all over it.

In THE MESSAGE, this verse reads: "This is the kind of love we're talking about—not that we once upon a time loved God, but that He loved us and sent His Son . . ."

When my husband Mark was pursuing me, he had already made up his mind about how he wanted it all to turn out. One day he looked me in the eye and said with sweet sincerity: "I have decided that you are the one for me. I will wait till you make up your mind. But I just want you to know, you don't have to do a thing."

Wow. The pressure was off of me to try and win his heart. It was won. He already loved me. I didn't need to go through hoops or hide my flaws.

That's the way it is with God. He already wanted us. We were born being loved by Him.

That's the ultimate welcome—to be loved before we step into the room—to know that once we get inside, we'll be welcomed with open arms. This is God's hospitality.

They say that timing is everything. If that's the case, God got it timed just right when He got the table set for our coming. The Bible says it best: "You see, at just the right time, when we were still powerless, Christ died for the ungodly . . . God demonstrates His own love for us in this: while we were still sinners Christ died for us" (Romans 5:6,8). He knew what kind of guests He was dealing with, and He still invited us to come. And He allowed His Son to die so that we could.

### He's Set a Place For Us

How else can we know that God has a welcoming heart and that we are included in His welcome?

The beloved shepherd's Psalm 23 gives us a clue:

"You prepare a table before me . . . and I will dwell in the house of the Lord forever"

When we know that company's coming, we get prepared—maybe even bake a cake, set an extra place, get another chair. And if we don't have time to dust, we can just dim the lights and light a candle.

God knew we were coming, and He got ready. He prepared a place for us right next to Him. He knew ahead of time just what we would need—a meal, comfort in our circumstances, rest from fear, a clean slate, a true home that would last forever.

God welcomed us long ago to His table. He wanted our company. We might get company we don't necessarily want (but we won't tell anyone that's how we're feeling!)

James 4:8 tells us that we can "draw near to God." We all get the best seat, and it's always by Him. He's constantly prepared for our coming. He keeps the door ajar, anticipating—eagerly expecting—our arrival, maybe checking at the window to see if we're on our way.

I read about a new book on foster parenting called *Another Place at the Table* by Kathy Harrison. What a wonderful title. Who doesn't want to know there's room at the table, no matter how many have already arrived, no matter what your condition upon arrival? The author explained her passion for taking in children in need of a temporary home: "I loved the feeling of having another chance to get it right for a child."

Whoever comes to God's table not only gets a place to sit, but a place to stay. He's made another place at the table. And through Christ, He's given us another chance to get it right. The table is long enough for all who will say yes to His invitation.

He adopts us as His children, and it's forever. The Bible says if we believe in Him we become His very own children (see John 1:12). We'll never have to move on, we'll never have to wonder where we'll spend our next night or eat our next meal. God becomes our parent, and it's permanent.

He's prepared a place for us and there's room for more.

When I was nine years old, my oldest brother left home rebellious, bitter, and cynical. He spent ten years running away from his upbringing and God. One day, in a motel in Mexico, he read about God's welcome one more time, and he decided to RSVP for good and become a member of God's family. When we all heard about it, we were more than amazed. Who would have ever thought the black sheep would return to the fold? We welcomed him with much joy and celebration. Our family still marks that day as the most astonishing miracle in our family. And my brother would agree. He once was lost, but then was found. And God was at the door, waiting, arms open wide.

God's welcome heart is best shown in a story of another wayward son and his father. Jesus tells this parable in Luke 15. After a rebellious teenager runs away from home, squanders all his money, and ends up eating with the pigs, he decides to come home, hoping at least for a better meal.

His dad catches a glimpse of him turning into the driveway and he tears out the front door, runs down the road, grabs him and kisses him. He calls out to everyone, "Let's celebrate. My son is home—he was once dead and is alive again, he was lost and is found." What a party they had, and no greater welcome!

We, too, are lost, in need of a home, in need of life— and God, like that father, is looking out the front door, keeping it open, checking to see if we're on our way home. The table is set, the extra chair is there. He's ready and waiting. And whoever turns into God's driveway will find Him running to meet him/her first, arms outstretched.

That's God's welcome. That's God's heart. No matter where you've been, no matter how long you've been gone, the door's open, and there's room for you inside.

## We're All Invited

God's invitation included the whole world. He let us know that fact over and over again, to whole groups, to individuals who sought Him out, to us who read His Word.

One cold and clear night, a bunch of stunned and bewildered shepherds heard the news first. An angel declared, "I bring you good news of great joy that shall be for all people." No exclusivity there. God was preparing to host the whole world through His Son, not only that group of men who first heard the news. They just got to hear it first. But the good news was for "all people," and God did the inviting to that first baby shower. The angels told them to get down to that manger and worship that baby because He was going to be their Savior.

God's invitations kept right on coming. Jesus assured an earnest seeker named Nicodemus that he, too, was included in the invitation: "For God so loved the world . . ." (John 3:16) And Peter comforts his readers with the assurance that God doesn't want anyone to die separated from Himself (see 2 Peter 3:9).

All people, the whole world, anyone and everyone—we're all invited. Just being born puts your name on His guest list. He hosts the "Open Arms Inn," and His invitation includes you and me.

Early in our marriage, I was listing off all the people I wanted to have over to our house. A little overwhelmed, Mark exclaimed, "You don't have to invite the whole world . . . at least by next month." He was right. But God did welcome the world, a world that includes you and me.

We know that because He created us when He didn't have to. He loved us first so that we would know how to love. He got everything ready in preparation for our coming. He looked out the door to see if we were on our way. He made room for us at the table.

And He made sure we knew we were all invited.

Why be hospitable? Because God is a welcoming God.

~~

◀❈▶

# Creamy Risotto

**1 medium onion, diced**

**½ cup butter, divided**

**1 cup rice**

**1 ¾ cup to 2 cups consommé or beef broth**

**½ cup sherry or white wine**

**½ cup grated fresh Parmesan**

**¾ cup frozen peas (opt.)**

**Ham or cooked chicken (opt.)**

Sauté onion in ¼ cup butter in large skillet until soft. Add rice and stir until rice turns yellow. Add broth and sherry. Bring to boil, then reduce heat. Cover and let summer 15 - 20 minutes. Add remaining ¼ cup butter and stir in cheese. Makes 6 servings easily.

I made this in the morning, except for the cheese. I warmed it up after work, added a bit more liquid, cheese, peas and ham - heated until the peas were cooked but still bright green and crunchy. Enjoy!

# Chapter 5

# God's Invitation

Before the table was set, the invitation was sent.

I want to invite you to one of the most beautiful spots in San Luis Obispo, California, the *Apple Farm Inn*. Maybe you've experienced its charms.

It's lovely. Somehow the flowers are always blooming, the coffee's always hot, and if, by chance you're sitting in a corner waiting for your name to be called, you'll never find dust on the furniture or spots on the window.

It seems even God and the weather cooperate as the sun slants just the right way through any window or the shifting clouds beyond the creek add a cozy warmth through the cheery curtains.

I imagine much thought and energy made the Apple Farm what it is: a business designed to make people feel at home. A place to which you feel personally invited and welcomed to return again and again. I wish it were my home! One time, while helping someone check into the Inn, I sat down in one of the lobby's wingback chairs and began welcoming the guests as they entered one by one—

"Come in," I said. "Welcome! Have a seat. Would you care for some coffee or hot cider?"

I enjoyed this lovely and short-lived bit of fantasy, especially the part about no dust.

Even the flag hanging from the porch roof is never faded. Changed often, I imagine. A minor detail, yet all part of an inviting atmosphere designed to welcome all who pass through their doors.

## Our Banner of Welcome

God understands this kind of hospitality and preparation and attention to detail. He is the Ultimate Host. He revealed His welcoming heart when He sent His Son, Jesus, to a world without hope.

Jesus is His beautiful invitation.

The banner from heaven's porch, also never faded, has a blood-stained cross sewn into its royal fabric. God has flown His banner of invitation down through the ages and it reads: "Your sins can be forgiven, you can know Me by name. Your despair can turn to hope; your life can have purpose and joy and peace. And it's all at My table. Come and know My Son."

## Imperfect Guests, Wrong Clothes

God created the world and said it was good. He was the Perfect Host, and for a short time, we were the perfect guests. But at the Fall, sin entered the world, and for all generations to come, we needed to know how to get back to His table.

Somehow we were never quite dressed for the occasion. God needed us to wear holiness; and no matter what we put on, we just couldn't meet that standard. He knew that, so along with the invitation, He sent the right wardrobe—the righteousness of His

Son. His banner said it all. Once we believe that Jesus died for us, we are forgiven. God sees us in His Son's perfect clothes, and we are more than welcome at His side, into His family. We are His very own children. He wanted us all along; we just needed to know what to wear.

Our clothing couldn't be just anything. Our good deeds were never good enough, and our good intentions failed far too often. The Bible says that God "dressed me up in a suit of salvation, He outfitted me in a robe of righteousness" (Isaiah 61:10, *THE MESSAGE*). And Paul adds that of course we couldn't find these clothes on our own, no matter how hard we tried: "Our righteousness, holiness, and redemption are in Christ Jesus—so there's no room to brag about how great you look without Him" (1 Corinthians 1:30-31 –*THE MESSAGE*).

Last spring one of the prodigals in our family came home and experienced those precious robes of righteousness in a beautiful way.

My niece Allison had wandered a bit from the fold in her early twenties. She came to live with her folks in between jobs, destitute in spirit and pocket. God used a book and a revival going on in my brother's church to continue to invite her to Himself. Shortly before she was going back to L.A., she RSVP'd to her heavenly Father's invitation and became His own with a passion.

Her dad was the brother I mentioned who had been our family's prodigal so many years before. He knew how it felt to leave and then to return. And he knew that something special should be done to celebrate her homecoming. He told her, "Remember how when the Prodigal Son returned home, his father threw him a great party? Well, he also gave his son his best robes. We don't have time to throw you a party, but let's go shopping for some new clothes!" And they did.

Allison told me she had to calm her dad down, knowing they didn't have much in the way of finances. He'd say, "It fits, it's beautiful, buy another one!" She said to me, "Aunt Sue, I felt like I didn't deserve them. They were too fine a quality."

Isn't that how we feel when we recognize where we've come from? We don't deserve Christ's righteousness, yet that's our clothing. "You are all sons of God through faith in Christ Jesus, and have clothed yourselves with Christ" (Galatians 3:27).

There is no finer quality than God's grace through Christ. And it's all part of the invitation. We're dressed in Him and by Him. When we believe that, we are on our way home.

## The Great Invitations of God

The best part of any written invitation is what's inside the envelope.

We can imagine a series of engraved invitations on the finest vellum, each beginning with:

"The pleasure of your company is requested.

Come to Me. You will find life, love, forgiveness and peace,"

—signed, God

~~

Our first invitation is to life itself.

When I was in college, I had a plaque on my wall that read: "Don't wait 'til you're in a desert before you learn to enjoy water." The funny thing is that the human condition is a desert. We need water on a regular basis. Without it, we die.

God knew that. Listen to the prophet Isaiah's joyful invitation to life and fulfillment:

"Hey, there! All who are thirsty, *come to the water*! Are you penniless? *Come anyway.* Why do you spend your money on junk food? Listen to me, listen well: Eat only the best, fill yourself with only the finest. *Come close now*, listen carefully to my life-giving, life-nourishing words. I'm making a lasting covenant commitment with you . . . sure, solid, enduring love" (Isaiah 55:1-3, *THE MESSAGE*).

We "come" for water—for life itself. We "come anyway," even if we have nothing to pay for it, which is true of all of us. And, we need to "come close" and listen to His promised words of hope and love.

Because we are created to know God, we will have perpetual thirst until we do.

"Come and drink," He says. God uses circumstances in our lives to remind us to come to His well to get our thirst quenched. A loved one lets us down; we don't get the promotion we anticipated; our health surprises us with bad news. God gets our attention the quickest when life throws us unwanted curves. It's then that we can see we've been drinking at the wrong well to satisfy our souls. We spend our time and money on the world's "junk food"—things like possessions, power, status, and relationships. We come to the end of these counterfeit "water" wells and wonder why we still thirst.

I remember a time when, after enduring a broken relationship, a friend said to comfort me: "What you need is a new boyfriend!" That sounded great! But, I knew it was just a quick fix. I had just read Psalm 62:5: "May my expectation be only in You, O God." (KJV) People are good—great even—but only when we look to God to slake our thirst will the holes in our soul be filled.

Real life comes from drinking at God's well. Jesus called it "living water," and when we drink of it, we won't have to go anywhere else. He said this to a woman who had spent too much time at the wrong well: "Whoever drinks the water I give him will never thirst . . . springing up to eternal life." (John 4:14).

~~

Next, we are invited to come to God so that we can know Him.

This second "welcome" is presented in John 1:46. Jesus had just told Philip to follow Him. Philip immediately went to Nathaniel and said, "We have found the Messiah, Jesus of Nazareth." Nathaniel's cryptic response was, "Can any good thing come out of Nazareth?" (from Barstow? from L.A.?)

Philip's simple answer changed Nathaniel's life: "Come and see." Come and see for yourself, Nathaniel. He did. He came to Jesus, saw who He was, and his immediate response was: "You are the Son of God, You are the King of Israel."

What's our invitation? We are invited to "come and see." We are invited to study God, learn about Him, listen to Him, and find out who He really is. How can we do that when He is God, and we are not? How can He so freely invite us to come and see Him? The answer is the cross. Remember that blood-stained fabric on our banner of welcome? There was nothing you or I could do about our sin. God knew we needed a Savior so that we could accept His invitation.

I was in a courtroom once, watching an innocent man being accused and slandered. I felt so helpless. I wanted to stand up and say, "Hey! That's a bunch of baloney. These accusations are false. I know this person. What you are hearing is not at all true."

But it wasn't my place to speak up. It was the place of the defense attorney. He was brilliant. He came to the defendant's rescue, even though the accused could do nothing. I sat there and watched this lawyer become the accused's advocate, presenting his case before the judge and jury. And the truth won out. I couldn't have done it; my friend had no voice, but he won because he had a great lawyer who knew what he was doing.

That's when I realized in a new way what Christ did for me. He was my advocate even when I was guilty. Jesus presented Himself before His holy Father, the righteous Judge, and said:

"I paid for Sue's sin. See the blood? See my wounds? Her debt is paid. My punishment was for her. Now she can be welcomed into the Family." And God agreed. He agreed to let me come and see Him, become His child, linger at His side and call Him "Abba, Father," my daddy (Romans 8:15).

Here is God's welcoming heart. He invites us into intimate relationship with Himself. We can "come and see" as much as our human minds can comprehend of Him this side of heaven. The journey to know God is an unending one, but it's one He's invited all of us to begin.

~~

We are invited to rest.

In his year-long devotional classic, My Utmost for His Highest, Oswald Chambers wrote (see June 11): "The questions that matter in life are remarkably few, and they are all answered by the words, 'Come unto Me.'"

Jesus answered all of our questions with that next great "welcome" of God in Matthew 11:28: "Come to Me, all who are weary and heavy-laden, and I will give you rest."

I love this. Who doesn't want rest?

I remember a time when I needed rest badly, and I thought I would never make it. I was in the middle of missionary training in Papua New Guinea, and had been sleeping in jungle huts for three nights. My days were spent trudging up and down steep paths with a pack on my back. At times I was literally sliding from tree to tree down the steep, muddy inclines to break my downhill speed. Earlier in my training, I had accidentally sliced a friend's arm with a machete as we were trying to cut down some tapioca plant and we were standing too close to each other. I had a certain reputation while on this hike. My guide took away my machete while I continued to slide down the hillsides.

At the end of the three-day trek, I remember finally almost stumbling into the camp. I slipped off my pack and made my way over to the group kitchen. The women with young children had stayed at home during our journey and they were busy making a hot lunch for us. I walked up to them and said, "I'm home," and burst into tears. I was exhausted (and probably in the best shape physically in my whole life).

They gathered around me like sympathetic hens and welcomed me back. I needed rest, and I got it at long last. (Of course, now that I'm a mother, I realize that they needed the rest more than I did!)

Jesus said we are to come to Him, and when we do, we find our rest. Rest doesn't only mean something physical like a good night's sleep. It means to come to a stop. Stop depending on our own strength and depend on God's. Stop depending on our own ideas of how to reach God, and rely on Christ. Stop thinking we can handle the weight of our responsibilities, problems, and pain. When we come to Jesus, we can stop any anxious fears in our future and give them to Him.

I heard former pastor of Menlo Park Presbyterian Church, Walt Gerber, say, "The main responsibility of a Christian is yieldedness."

Jesus is our rest stop where we can yield our very selves. We can do that even when we are limp with exhaustion or tied in knots from stress or worry. The rest He promises is relationship and peace with God. *THE MESSAGE* says it best:

"Get away with Me and you'll recover your life. I'll show you how to take a real rest. Walk with Me and work with Me, watch how I do it. Learn the unforced rhythms of grace. I won't say anything heavy or lay anything heavy or ill-fitting on you. Keep company with Me and you'll learn to live freely and lightly" (Matthew 11:28-30, *THE MESSAGE*).

~~

Jesus is the great invitation of God. Without Him, there is no invitation. With Him, our thirst is quenched, we see who God is, and at His table, we rest from fear and worry. "Christ is the centerpiece of everything we believe" (Hebrews 3:1, *THE MESSAGE*).

Through Him, God has said to us to come and drink, come and see, come and rest.

And we are all invited.

Why be hospitable? Because God first invited us to Himself.

~~

# Bev's Chocolate Zucchini Bread

¾ c. butter, softened

2 c. sugar

3 eggs

2 ½ c. flour

2 ½ tsp. baking powder

1 ½ tsp. baking soda

1 tsp. cinnamon

½ tsp. salt

⅔ c. cocoa

2 tsp. vanilla

2 ½ c. grated zucchini (skin and all)

½ c milk

1 c. chopped nuts

Cream butter and sugar. Beat in eggs. Combine all ingredients, stir well until blended. Spoon into two greased and floured loaf pans. Bake at 350° for 40 to 50 minutes. I had a salad topping mix of dried cranberries and pecans, so I threw in half a cup, along with chocolate chips, of course!

# Chapter 6

# God's Example

Hospitality includes two main ingredients: the host and the guest. It also involves some initiative by one or the other; usually the host, though not always.

Grace felt at home enough in my house, she walked right in and put the kettle on. She was my host in my house since she made the tea and I stopped what I was doing to join in. And, that was fine with me. Speaking of tea, hospitality may also include some sort of provision, whether it is something to drink, a snack, a full meal or just a listening ear.

One morning, a friend called to say she was feeling blue, so I invited her over. I, too, felt stressed, but it had more to do with the tornado-like condition of our under-the-stairs closet. By the time lunchtime had arrived, both of our needs had been met. We talked through her problems and sorted through mine, and we didn't have to pay a therapist or a professional organizer. A celebration over tuna sandwiches and tomato soup seemed appropriate.

Hospitality provides all kinds of needs for friends, or even strangers. God welcomes all strangers as friends at His table, and He knows what each one needs—food, drink—or, fellowship of a deeper kind.

# 7 Lessons from the Ultimate Host

Jesus met a stranger in the middle of a desert one afternoon. We never find out her name, but we see hospitality at its best. And the good china or linens were never even mentioned (read it for yourself in John 4:1-7). Here are some details.

Jesus and His disciples were headed north from Judea to Galilee. He led the way through a place called Samaria. Now, Jews and Samaritans hated each other, and normally they would go miles out of their way to keep their distance. Instead, Jesus went straight through Samaria.

The disciples were probably wondering just why they had to go that route. But Jesus had God's agenda on His mind, and it had to do with His guest list. Salvation was for everyone—even women, who stood on the last rung of everyone's social ladder of that time

Jesus set out to show His Father's welcome through this encounter with the now famous woman at the well.

## Lesson 1: It's God's Guest List

The first lesson in hospitality: to be God's invitation to the world, we may have to walk through unfamiliar territory and invite the unexpected guest.

We all have people in our world who are easy to include. We can't get enough of them. Then there are the others. They are different. We feel awkward around them. We are not inclined to serve them, much less welcome them to our table and into our lives.

But, God has invited the world, and that includes both kinds of guests. We need to ask: "Is God's invitation supposed to come through me?"

Who would have thought that this woman at the well would ever become a follower of Jesus? And she brought half her village with her. She definitely fit under the category of "least likely to become a Christian." Who do you have in your life that could make that list? Maybe a relative, your child's teacher, a retail clerk you've befriended, a lonely college student, your husband, your ex-husband?

Have they been offered the gift of living water? Do they know who Jesus is because you are in their life? You may need to have them for tea. Perhaps being at your table is the closest they've ever been to knowing Jesus loves them. It'll take work, but it's worth the effort.

As you know, needy persons aren't always dressed in rags. They may even dress better than you do. So keep your eyes and ears open, and invite someone to His table, even if you have to go off the beaten path.

~~

## Lesson 2: It's God's Timing

A second lesson in hospitality: we can trust God's timing (or, life's an adventure with God!)

Jesus knew it was time to get out of Judea. He didn't grouse about it. He took it in stride and used the opportunity to help a thirsty woman.

I like to be in control, to know what's going to happen next and just how much time I have to make it happen. Don't you feel that way? Especially when it comes to inviting people into your home, people you may not even know, for heaven's sake (even when it is for heaven's sake)!

We women are planners. We need to get our ducks in a row. Some of us have more ducks than others. We like to make sure we have enough food, enough time, enough energy. We'd like to know that the kids will behave, that the guests won't stay too late, that our husbands won't fall asleep in the middle of the evening or whatever our particular angst of the moment.

But can we relax when things don't go as planned? That's a tough one. But we have a God who sees the big picture.

The disciples had their doubts, but Jesus never left the controls.

Can we trust that He knows what He's doing even if the coffee pot breaks at the last minute or a surprise guest arrives an hour later than everyone else? Will we let Him be God in the unexpected?

God may be saying to you, "Listen to Me. I want to invite the world to Myself. You may have to walk through Samaria – oh, well! Why don't you ask that person today, and I will take care of the details."

Next time the unexpected occurs, or the guest list changes at the last minute, it could be quite exciting—fun, even—to see how God helps you serve someone He's had His eye on for a while. He really is in charge. In spite of all your lists of what to do when, His timetable is the only one worth following. Are you looking for more adventure in your life? Invite someone over and enjoy the ride.

~~

In John 4:7, Jesus' first words to this woman were: "Will you give me a drink?" Sounds like she was the one offering the hospitality.

Why didn't He just tell her straight up, "Look, I'm exactly what you've been looking for all along. Today is the best day of your life. God has come to you in the flesh. Now pay close attention to what I have to say."

Instead, He asked her to meet His need. He was thirsty, and she could help.

## Lesson 3: We are to Invite and Receive

Lesson number 4: we can invite others to Jesus by showing we have needs, too.

Former president of Multnomah Bible College and author, Joe Aldrich, calls this "presenting the gift of our own needs."

One day, a neighbor casually mentioned that I was the one who fed the whole neighborhood. (Not true, but that's how he perceived me.) Is that how people saw me, always helping others. but never needing any help? I made sure he brought the pie next time he came over!

The point is this: It is a gift to show others that we need them, too. It puts us on a level playing field. They can hear our words about God easier when they realize we can't do it alone. We all need God. All of us are thirsty without Him. We must all drink daily from His well; and without Him, we're all the same: hungry, lonely, without eternal purpose or lasting relationships.

The next time a new friend offers to help, accept readily, and see how God deepens your relationship for His sake.

~~

I love how Jesus directs the next part of their conversation. He shows us that hospitality is so much more than food and drink. We may think it consists only of host, guest, and provision. But doesn't God have more in mind? We offer a cup of tea to a friend and then, along with it, something of who He is—a gift of friendship, a word of comfort, a moment of truth.

## Lesson 4: It's a Door to Deeper Sharing

Lesson number 4: hospitality begins on the surface but often goes much deeper.

This woman at the well wondered aloud how Jesus could ask her for a drink, and He immediately went to the next level: "If you knew the gift of God and who it is that asks you for a drink, you would have asked him and he would have given you living water" (John 4:10) He adds the immortal lines, "The one who drinks the water I give Him will never thirst again" (v.11).

Whatever that meant, she knew she wanted it—more water and less work. What she didn't understand was that He had much more to offer than an easier lifestyle and her own personal drinking fountain. Jesus raised the stakes, and she sensed that this could be the beginning of something new and great and satisfying.

We can do the same thing. We offer our guest what God has given us, however He directs the conversation.

The other day around our table, a young hairdresser said to me: "Oh, I've been on my own since I was 15." Amazed, I just said, "Danielle, do you realize that God has done a great job of taking care of you these last several years?"

"Yes, I know that very well," she responded. For that brief moment, we were reminded of our Shepherd's care, and the path opened to a deeper relationship.

Another word for hospitality could be "alongside-ness." God draws us alongside. Then we pass His strength on to others. Second Corinthians 1:4 tells us how: "God comes alongside us when we go through hard times, and before you know it, He brings us alongside someone else who is going through hard times so that we can be there for that person just as God was there for us" (*THE MESSAGE*).

We may offer a hot meal, or perhaps a bed for a night or two, but that can be just the beginning. May our guests encounter truth and relationship at our table; it can be a matter of simply asking the right questions and allowing God to answer their questions.

Hospitality includes preparation. Sometimes we need to change the bed sheets, get out the cloth napkins or fix a special entrée. But what our company truly needs is a bit of grace from Jesus—spontaneous and overflowing from hearts filled with Him.

Jesus knew the kind of life the Samaritan woman was leading. She had been drinking at the cracked well of broken relationships for many years. She hadn't faced the fact that leaking wells can't fill you up. It took her a moment or two to realize that Jesus was offering what she wanted.

Only an honest person will admit there's more to life than what the world delivers. Even then, he or she may not take what God gives. If you offer someone living water and he refuses, he may just go ahead and spend more time drinking at different wells.

~~

## Lesson 5: It Reflects the Giver of Living Water

Lesson number 5: we don't have all the answers to another's problems. We just offer God's Living Water. A person chooses to drink or not. We simply need to be that clear, flowing channel of His grace and mercy. The more consistently *we* drink, the clearer our channel.

Someone said, "Ministry is spillage." Are we so filled with God that He automatically spills over onto the people in our lives?

At first, this story seems to be about a woman's hospitality to Jesus—He was asking her for a drink. But it quickly switches to God's hospitality to her. He becomes the host when He offers her an eternal gift.

We experience a certain interchangeability of hospitality. God invites us to come to Him, and we in turn welcome Him into our lives. When He knocks on our door, we invite Him in: "Lord, make Yourself at home in me. I am at Your service."

If He wants a glass of water—or whatever—we don't ask questions, we just give it to Him.

Here a woman had an opportunity to literally give a cup of water to our Lord but she was blinded by her own need. She was tired of walking to that well. Her life was hard, and hardened by her own choices. She couldn't even think about hosting Jesus, even if it was only with a glass of water.

Isn't that sometimes the way it is with us? We are concentrating on how our needs aren't getting met. We may be scurrying around, trying to make sure they do, even if it means ignoring the very guests God has sent us. And we don't listen to our Master's request that might sound like this:

"Sue, you need to give this person a cup of water in my name, and you aren't even listening. I know you are stressed. Let Me take care of you. You take care of My sheep."

I find it very hard to feed His sheep when I'm feeling sorry for myself. We can't offer God's welcome to someone else if we haven't yet welcomed God into our lives.

~~

### Lesson 6: Deeper Offerings

Lesson number 6:  we are to offer the eternal alongside the meal. Do you serve what's truly important at your table? Is your priority the material or the spiritual? Do you "serve God" along with the salad and the potatoes at every meal? That can be far more significant than any menu.

My sister told me once: "Every night, try to have something green on your plate." She meant it for nutrition and color.

I try. I serve lima beans and peas and spinach and green salad and Blue Lake green beans. I've given up on zucchini. The kids fight it all the way, but someday they will like at least one of those healthy and pretty things, I'm fairly certain.

My purpose is to feed them well, whether or not they recognize the value of green, or any other color. But besides good vitamins, I need to serve them a God who loves and forgives, and provides purpose for their lives. And they will see it best when I am living it out. I'd better make sure they see a mother who rejoices and relaxes in doing her Father's will. That's a nutrition that will hold them in good stead and guide them to eternity.

In the story of the Samaritan woman, Jesus shared His worldview with His disciples: "Open your eyes and look at the fields. They are ripe for the harvest" (John 4:35). He served them what was important and would sustain them along the way. With God's help, our guests can leave our company meal blessed as well as fed, sustained in heart, soul and body.

~~

Hospitality is hard work. Jesus knew that for a fact and He told His followers in John 4:36-38 that some will sow, and some will reap; it all takes effort.

My brother Steve is a pastor, and when his wife's brother died suddenly, he led the memorial service. The room was full. Bill wasn't a believer, as far as we know, nor was most of his family. Steve had an opportunity to plant some spiritual seeds, and everyone heard the gospel clearly.

It was tricky, being family and all, so he started by saying: "I'm a pastor, so you might expect me to say something religious—which I will—but first I want to talk about Bill. He made me want to be a better man."

Steve went on to say the Bible stands for: "Basic Instructions Before Leaving Earth." Steve was a sower. He said later that he didn't think the family appreciated all that he said. He didn't get much earthly reward. It was hard work; but we don't really know whose life may have been changed as a result of that effort. His job was to be faithful to the task. And so is ours.

## Lesson 7: Don't Look for a Reward

The seventh lesson: hospitality takes effort, and sometimes you see results and sometimes you don't. But that shouldn't keep us from doing the work, sowing that seed and presenting the food God offers. Jesus gives life and hope and eternity to those who believe in Him, even the most unlikely guest.

God's hospitality is summed up in John 6:35: "I am the bread of life. He who comes to Me will not hunger, and he who believes in Me will never thirst."

Jesus took His hospitality to everyone He met. He made the conversation go deeper to reveal the true heart needs. And He said the harvest is ripe for the picking.

He will bring people to our table and into our lives so that we can offer His cup of living water and His bread of life. That's a great life purpose; it's our very meat. And we are blessed.

Why be hospitable? Because God invited the world to Himself, including you.

~~

# Lynnel's Spinach Noodle Casserole

1 ½ lbs. hamburger

½ t. each salt and pepper

2 cloves garlic, minced

26 oz. spaghetti sauce

1 t. Italian seasoning

10 oz. chopped frozen spinach, thawed and drained

2 c. Monterey Jack cheese, grated

1 ½ c. sour cream

1 egg

1 t. garlic salt

8 oz. wide egg noodles, cooked (5-6 cups dry noodles)

1 ½ c. shredded Parmesan cheese

Cook and drain meat, salt and pepper and garlic. Add sauce and Italian seasoning to meat. Combine spinach, Monterey Jack cheese, sour cream, egg, garlic salt, and noodles.

In greased 9x13 pan, layer: noodle mixture, ½ of the Parmesan cheese, beef and sauce, then remaining Parmesan. Bake at 350° for 40 minutes or until bubbly.

# The Favor of a Reply Is Requested

## The Invitation

"I have swept away your offenses like a cloud, your sin like the morning mist. Return to Me, for I have redeemed you" (Isaiah 44:22, NIV).

"Come on over, I've set a place for you— and there's one for your friend— Why don't you ask her, too?"

## The RSVP

Lord,

What a welcome! Nothing can compare with it. I'm not sure why it seems so new to me. I thought I knew You all these years. Somehow I missed this—You invited me to know You, sit with You, be treated like a special guest and loved as Your closest friend.

I accept. (Can I do that? Just "accept"? Okay, I will.)

I accept the staggering fact that You wanted me to come to You. I'm Yours now. And I thank You.

Now what is it You want me to do?

Write *your* RSVP:

# Part III

# Using Your Home for God's Welcome

## *Prologue*

"A dining room table with children's eager, hungry faces around it, ceases to be a mere dining room table and becomes an altar." —Simeon Strunsky

Lord, really? My table an altar? Have you seen my table?

(*Actually, I have.*)

~~

"Compulsion keeps a sparkling house. But love and prayer stand a better chance of producing a happy family." —James Hewitt

I do love a happy family— even more than a sparkling house— although both would be great. Clean or not, how can I welcome the world to You in my home?

(*Just try, one step at a time. I'll help. It's My table, after all.*)

~~

"At this feast it is He Who has spread the board and it is He Who has chosen the guests." —C. S. Lewis

Okay, then, I'm convinced of this: God welcomed me. It's time I welcome others. I can't do it without You, though . . .

*(I know that better than you. I'll give the strength and grace you need. And your guest list, and your menu, and all the other details. Just ask.)*

# Chapter 7

# Tried and True Tips (for the Truly Tired)

### Breakfast for Dinner

My folks lived in a house trailer during Dad's last two years of college. Dad was making forty-three cents an hour, and they were barely scrimping by. One afternoon, some friends came to visit, and they stayed and stayed. Mom wished they'd go home because she was hungry and had no idea what to serve her guests.

Finally, her friend said, "Betty, I'm hungry, let's fix something!"

"I am, too," Mom said, "but I don't know what to fix."

Her guest asked, "Do you have bacon?"

"Yes," my mom replied.

"Bread? Eggs?"

She did have all those things. "Okay, then let's make toast and eggs and bacon." That day, Mom learned that things could be simple, that folks didn't care about being impressed with some

91

great feast. It was the friendship that counted, the time together that mattered.

Although your paycheck is a little better than forty-three cents an hour, you still might feel it's not enough to add another mouth at the table. Not only that, but your calendar may already be packed, your to-do list is off the page, and your merry-go-round life shows no sign of stopping. Doing hospitality may seem like just one more thing to add to a strained and stretched schedule. I'm surprised you even had time to read this page. Maybe you are, too.

We've all felt that way at some time. An overfull schedule can become a way of life. To add "having company" might just be too much to think about. Yet, you still want to pass on God's welcome heart. The good news is that He's promised to help.

God calls His help "the unforced rhythms of grace" (Matthew 11:29, *THE MESSAGE*). He doesn't want our lives so crowded and crunched; He will help us clear our time table to do what He wants us to do. He invites us to work alongside Him, offer the invitation and learn to do it without the stress and strain. Take a moment now to ask: "Lord, how can I do this when I'm already too busy? Please show me what to do. Amen."

God doesn't command something that He doesn't give us the strength to do. When the doorbell rings, we can say over and over, walking toward the door: "I can do all things through Christ who strengthens me" (Philippians 4:13). Taking risks for God is an exciting way to live—and what a testimony to His power when we do something we're scared to do, or when we swallow our pride and just do it! Bacon and eggs is a good way to begin, at any time of day.

## Hints for the Hesitant

How do you get started when you feel shy, tired, broke or inexperienced? You might think, "Hey, she's an outgoing person and has a million friends [or a million dollars]. Of course, it's easy for her." The truth is, everyone has her own set of challenges. Mom's challenges were a tight budget and lack of experience. Your challenge may be not knowing when to fit it in or what to serve. Even the most accomplished hostess has moments of self-doubt.

Here are some tried-and-true tips that have helped me, and others, make the effort in spite of doubts or anxieties. I've divided the tips into five categories, but some overlap. As you read them, you may think of other ideas. Try one this week and see if it makes a difference in how you offer God's welcome in your home.

## Preparing Your Home

*Be willing to have people see you as you are, because then they will feel more comfortable to be themselves in return.* --Lori Payton, hosting in Chicago in her fourteenth kitchen

**TIP** - No time to dust? Dim the lights and use candlelight. The guests will never notice and the ambiance will be lovely.

**TIP** - Buy paper goods in bulk or off-season. When you're tired but want to offer a sandwich to a lonely college student, you'll be happy you had that stack of paper plates and cups.

**TIP** - One woman told me that her mother never left the house without vacuuming first--just in case she came home with guests. That's one way to be prepared. Usually I'm in too much of a hurry to carry out that goal, but if the table is cleared (or the couch or the countertops), it does provide a nicer welcome for any surprise guest (and less stress for me!)

**TIP** – Enlist your family's help. If kids have regular chores, you can know that at least one day a week the house will be vacuumed and the trash taken out. Take advantage of that day and invite a friend over. If your children only see you slaving away at preparing for company, they may think it's too much work, and not something they want to do when they grow up. Try announcing a "Fast- 5-Minute-Frenzy" when everyone tidies up one space for five minutes. Amazing the amount of work that can be accomplished in such a short time. Working together is good for them and good for the home.

**TIP** - Find a convenient centerpiece—one that won't break with too much handling and doesn't have too many pieces to it unless it's all on a tray. The idea is to be able to clear the table and replace the centerpiece quickly. If you need to fix your home in an elaborate manner in order to have company, you won't have company; it's just too much trouble. One idea: cover a stain in the tablecloth with a wall mirror. Add a candle or two and pass the gravy! Once I used a queen -sized quilt to cover my table when I had some formal company. It added warmth and interest, looked great, and washed up fine. I've placed small potted plants in a large basket for a simple spot of color. When the flowers fade, you can replant them outside and you haven't wasted your money. Ask a gardening friend what kind of cut flowers would grow best around your home. Calla lilies grow like weeds almost year round in our shady front yard, and they are easy to cut at any length for the door basket or a vase on the table.

**TIP** - Move your dinnerware or china to a convenient location. I moved the good china recently just so that I would use it more often. If everything is packed away, we won't use it. When I was growing up, we got out the good china every Sunday. Mom always said, "China is meant to be used." (Mom isn't a formal person, she just likes pretty dishes—she has two china cabinets and would like another!) I don't remember much breakage, if any, and Mom enjoyed the beauty, as did our guests. Too many special dishes only get looked at rather than used, and without the use, there are no memories to go along with that special piece. Decorative, stacking plate racks can hold the pretty plates on the counter and are easily accessible for dinners or tea parties. I found a metal baker's rack at a discount store that holds nice dishes, trays, and cookbooks, and it sits near the table for easy access.

**TIP** – Speaking of china, it's good to learn your own décor personality. You might not "do china." That's perfectly okay. Find out what you do like, invest in three or four things over time that bring you pleasure in their beauty, and make your home reflect who you are. Get rid of things you don't need or enjoy (that teapot collection you inherited from Aunt Edna may be more enjoyed by a close friend who fell in love with it at first sight.)

**TIP** – Share sets of dishes with friends when you have a large company gathering. This idea also works well for borrowing large or unique cooking pans. There's no need for everyone to own everything, and it cuts down on storage problems.

**TIP** – Pretty dishes are cheaper than paper, if you have the time to wash them. However, sometimes paper is the way to go to ease the workload.

**TIP** – Choose a flower from your garden to decorate each place setting. Even a fern leaf looks pretty set by the plate. My friend Grace had a tiny house, but each time we came for tea or brunch, she would have an individual rose or candle placed by our cups. Simple touches, inexpensive, but sweet and special. Votives lit in extra teacups at each place setting are also pretty and inviting.

**TIP** – If you expect overnight guests, place potpourri in their room or light a scented candle for a while before they arrive. Once I arrived at a home in which I was to spend the night, and there on my bed was a basket filled with welcoming goodies: a mug, travel-sized soap and shampoo, and a washcloth. I felt like a queen, and my hostess loved planning it. She told me later how she frequented secondhand shops to buy one-of-a-kind china plates. For a dollar or two, she could find something pretty on which to place cookies to give away, and the plate was part of the gift! I began doing the same, sometimes finding teacups, as well, to fill with homemade jam and give to teachers and school secretaries.

TIP - If you wait until your house is perfect, you won't do have anyone over. My sister's pastor once asked his congregation: "Who left a messy house this morning when you came to church? Okay, everyone who raised their hand, invite someone home for sandwiches today after the service." He wanted to promote more community within his flock, and he was realistic about what real homes looked like (and the reasons why we don't have more people over).

TIP – Make your home welcoming, especially for first-time guests, by placing a balloon on the mailbox or a handmade "Welcome" sign on the front door. Even your little ones like the job of coloring this homemade welcome. Music is always festive or soothing, and it fills up any early blank spaces in the conversation.

TIP – Teach your family what to do when you get short notice for company coming. One friend calls it "Red Alert." Another friend calls out, "Mad Dash Time!" The kids know what needs to get done in short order, whether it's sweeping the front porch, wiping down the guest bathroom or changing the sheets. You not only get the much-needed help at the last minute, but your children also learn the importance of teamwork and how to make things special for guests. You might run through some practice times to provide the training for your kids, but that can be fun, too, if you add some valuable rewards. You can make banana splits or another special treat as they dash through the practice chores. Eventually, the reward is the pleasure their efforts bring you and your last-minute company.

**TIP** – Remember that hospitality can be a lot of work, often hard work. You develop your own cleanliness and preparation work quotient. Choose somewhere between what makes you comfortable and what makes you frazzled. Making all the beds before a ladies' coffee is not my idea of mandatory accomplishments (and hopefully no one will go upstairs during the morning). Your friends can help you keep a healthy balance if you are prone to not cleaning at all or going overboard with gourmet preparations for a two-year-old's birthday party. As you practice hospitality, you will discover your individual limits as to how much you can manage and what is important enough to you to expend the energy. And these limits can change over time.

## Preparing Your Food

*I had to learn that it's not so much what I cook on a limited budget, it's that I cook it with love.* —Quin Sherrer, *The Warm and Welcoming Home*, Regal Books

**TIP** - Use a tried-and-true, no-fail recipe, and keep the ingredients in the cupboard. If you don't have a recipe yet, ask a friend for her favorite, and try it out on your family and then on your friend's family.

**TIP** - If guests offer to bring something, take them up on it. It can put them at ease, and it helps you out with the expense and the planning. It may even save you a trip to the store. Keep in mind that your guest may also feel insecure about his or her cooking, so ask them if they would like to bring the salad or dessert or the bread (since they offered!) Even single guys can bring French bread and butter, and you can warm it when they arrive.

**TIP** - While menu planning, keep in mind that the dinner or snack is the vehicle to meeting the need in another person, not an end in itself. The pressure is off to make it ultra-gourmet or completely perfect when you remember that your guest needs you more than your food.

**TIP** - Use a crock pot with a removable crock. That way you can prepare the entrée the night before and place the crock in the refrigerator. (I've even done this with older models, cord and all.) Take it out and start it in the morning before work and you'll come home to a wonderful aroma and most of the meal completed. It makes it easy to invite a lonely coworker home for a yummy meal and family time.

**TIP**— If you're feeling energetic, plan company two or three nights in a row. The house will still be clean, you can use the same menu, and you only have to go to the store once.

**TIP** - Make Sunday dinner preparations on Saturday. Ask the Lord who needs an invite, and see whom He brings to mind or sits in the pew in front of you. Bring the person (or family) home with you. If they offer, they can stop at the store for ice cream on their way over.

**TIP** - Do ahead whatever you can. It will make you less tired and more able to concentrate on the needs of your guests. One friend sets the dining table a day in advance (only possible if you have two tables, of course). Many desserts freeze well and can be made days ahead of the event. Knowing that some of the work is already completed makes you more relaxed and your family less frazzled.

**TIP** – Along those same lines, when hamburger is on sale, divide and conquer. Spend 30 minutes browning the meat with chopped onion. Then divide it all in 1-lb. bags, and freeze. Use later for tacos, stroganoff, and enchilada casserole. My sister goes one step further and makes "taco meat", adding the seasonings before freezing to save that step later on.

**TIP** - Double your muffin or cookie recipes when possible. Freeze the extras for a last-minute coffee with a neighbor or coworker. Everyone loves homemade! Make a large-size bread in your bread machine and put it on dough cycle. Divide the dough and form in round loaves to bake in your oven. The crust is softer and you have one to give away or freeze for later.

TIP – Soups or stews feed a lot of people and are relatively inexpensive. When you add biscuits, French or sourdough bread to the menu, it's definitely company fare. One friend made homemade biscuits every night for a week until she perfected her craft. (I made them the other night and realized I need the practice as well!) She suggested that you learn to cook a few basic foods really well—things that your family likes a lot, such as yeast rolls, pancakes, BBQ, and so on. Then use them often to make the meal special. She added, "It doesn't have to be gourmet, but it's nice when it's delicious."

TIP – Keep cookie dough in the freezer, either rolled in wax paper or frozen in cookie-sized balls. Pop them out and bake right before company comes or while they are there. There's nothing like a chocolate chip cookie for dessert for any kind of gathering.

TIP – Find one thing you enjoy making and become an "expert" at making it. You can serve it at all your gatherings, and even receive a well-deserved reputation for being the best at your favorite food, whether it is an international appetizer or "secret family recipe" for deep, dark chocolate cake.

TIP – Keep ice cream in the freezer. If a cake flops, scoop it into bowls and cover it with ice cream. People will never know, and they may like it even better.

TIP - Give yourself permission to order out when you have more money than time. The great thing is you invited someone over. The menu is not the main event—although take-out might be just the treat your friends needed . . . and relationships flourish.

TIP – A quick way to dress up plain old hamburgers or hot dogs is to serve creative condiments on the side. Give your guests a choice to create their own memorable meal with interesting relishes, chutneys, salsa, olives or tapenades, and fancy mustards.

My dad always piled his burgers with crushed peanuts, and we ended up doing the same. ("Delish!" he would say, as he crunched into his mile-high burger.)

TIP – Bathe your meal preparation in prayer, and have fun!


## Preparing Your Family

*The home of a Christian is a tool for ministry. Ask the Lord how He wants you to use it.* —Karen Mains, *Open Heart, Open Home,* Mainstay Ministries

TIP – Since children learn by watching and doing, include your kids in the planning and preparation. They will learn the rewards of serving and gain confidence while doing it. Different jobs can be doled out to each child, appropriate to their age. I always filled the relish dishes with pickles and olives when I was little. As I got older, I could help with putting leaves in the table, getting out the good china, and peeling potatoes. Getting the kids in the kitchen for a group cleanup is fun and helpful, even though sometimes it takes longer because of a tea towel fight or two.

TIP – A child can develop confidence and joy from being the one who makes a special recipe for your dinner parties or family events. John loved Caesar Salad and learned how to make it. Now when his mom says, "Jono, company is coming and I need your salad," he knows exactly what to do, and she has one less thing to prepare. The recipe card in their family is entitled: "Jono's Salad." I'm sure he will enthrall his own family in the future with his flair in the kitchen, and he likes being the expert and source of blessing to others. Bonnie tried a new recipe for garlic green beans, and now we call it "Bonnie's green beans." And when it's anything different, everyone is disappointed.

**TIP** - My sister said that the more convenient our hospitality is, the more we we'll do it. Think about what makes it convenient for your family, and put that plan into action. Convenience often has to do with the family's schedule. If I know we will all be home on Sunday evening, I can ask someone over for an early supper, knowing also that I'll have the afternoon to prepare.

**TIP** - Ask your family whom they think could use an invitation to your home. They may suggest their best friends at first, unless they are already at the house all the time. Help your family consider who could be blessed by your home, a good meal or games around the table. Make a list and mark the calendar. Each child could help with the planning and preparing for the time when their special guest is scheduled.

**TIP** – The earlier you begin hospitality, the easier it will be for your kids when they are grown. Inviting others into their homes will be a natural part of their lifestyle because they watched you do it and enjoyed the process. Even if it's difficult for you, you want hospitality to be easier for them, so begin today.

**TIP** – Hospitality is not a competition (if you don't count racing to put away the vacuum before the doorbell rings). We naturally compare ourselves with one another, but there will always be someone with more money, better culinary skills, a bigger hot tubs (or, a hot tub) and a nicer sound system. But that's not hospitality, that's "Look at me, please be impressed . . . oh, and have a good time while you're here." Living and serving within our means is a great testimony to our kids that we can still love God and others and not go into debt. And we'll be doing it for the right reason.

**TIP** - So that your children learn the fun and blessing of hosting, invite their friends for tea and cookies. Teach them how to welcome guests at the door, how to introduce one another, and let the guest go "first."

**TIP** – When your children get a little older, make sure they know how to welcome guests, take their coats and offer something to drink. One mother, arriving home later than she expected, was relieved and pleased to see that her 16-year-old son had invited her friend in, offered some water and at least wondered if he should put out a bowl of almonds. He'd been trained, and he had been watching his mom. She was delighted, and so was her guest.

**TIP** – Sometimes there are hospitality "disasters," or things don't quite live up to your expectations. Our kids can learn from our mistakes—not only how not to make the same ones, but how to handle themselves in the face of them. When you remain relaxed if the rice is soggy or the centerpiece falls in the gravy, you can use the situation to highlight the real reason the guests are there: to show them how much God loves them. The emphasis is always on God, His love and the ones at your table experiencing that love. Humor and grace are a wonderful combination. The best gift you can give another person is the ability to laugh at yourself (and you can always cry later if it makes you feel better.)

**TIP** - Start a family tradition: BLTs on Saturday nights, waffles on Sunday nights, or chili and cornbread on Friday nights. Choose a favorite that is simple to make and easy to multiply. (See Chapter 8 for a yummy taco soup that's easy to double or triple.) If you know it's going to be effortless and a success, you can readily invite someone to join you, even at the last minute. Keep the ingredients on hand in the pantry or freezer. (You can even freeze chips, so buy extra when on sale.)

**TIP** – Invite families you want your children to know. I grew up knowing many adult friends of my parents. It's still difficult to call them by their first names. Mr. Elliott, Mrs. Nicholson, the Millers––all held a special place in my heart. My parents' hospitality provided a wonderful resource of mature people who loved and prayed me into my own adulthood. Now I want to give this same gift to our kids.

**TIP** – Teenagers need a place to hang out. If you have one or more teenagers, you know what an honor it is to have that place be your home (maybe not every night . . .) Food and games are usually a good enough incentive . . . and welcoming parent-hosts. Teach guys to make doughnuts; organize a chili cook-off; or make your own pizzas. Our friends make a chocolate chip cookie dough recipe-and-a-half to bake in a jelly roll pan. While still warm from the oven, and with a half-gallon of ice cream piled in the middle, eager teens begin spooning from all sides. They call it a "pazooki," and double dipping is definitely allowed. Make your home the fun place to be, and you will see your kids more often and become friends with their friends.

**TIP**—If your kids (or spouse) groan when you say, "Company's comin'," take time to listen to their complaints. If it's something legitimate, make the needed changes. Maybe you get too uptight and cause undue tension in the home. Maybe the timing's not right. However, if laziness, selfishness, or fear is the source of their moans, ask them for their input as to what they could do to develop a welcoming heart, and do it anyway!

**TIP** – Some events, like birthdays and anniversaries, are more exclusive, and only family is usually included. That kind of exclusivity helps develop family closeness and identity. Holidays can be more inclusive in nature to show God's welcome. Use holiday opportunities to include singles who may not have family nearby or even invite other families. Thanksgiving, Easter, and Christmas offer occasions to provide a special welcome for someone who needs your home and family. Christians can't afford to be exclusive this side of heaven.

**TIP** – Train your children how to speak to adults and other children. They enjoy role-playing with you as the honored guest. They can learn the basics of looking adults in the eye, speaking respectfully, saying their greetings and thank-yous, walking their friends to the door and saying their good-byes. I've had to prepare our kids and give needed reminders, but they also pick it up from hearing us do the same.

**TIP** – Have your kids (or grandkids) plan an annual anniversary dinner for family or close friends to celebrate everyone's special event. The kids can plan the menu, make placemats, help prepare food and help clean up. Take the opportunity to teach simple table manners and common courtesies. It's a big effort for you at first, but through the years, the children grow up, become more experienced and will do more on their own.

**TIP** – Hospitality doesn't always have to be at home. Take a batch of cookies and your kids over to an elderly neighbor. He or she will love the attention, and it's good for both generations. They might develop shared interests like stamp collecting and gardening. Every Easter the girls decorate cupcakes with jellybeans, make popsicle- stick crosses, and write: "Christ Is Risen" on paper plates. They leave these goodie plates on neighborhood doorsteps—offering a fun surprise and a good reminder to both young and old. I call it "Drive-by Hospitality," and it opens doors for future friendships.

## Preparing Your Time Together

*"Your love has given me great joy and encouragement because you, my brother, have refreshed the hearts of the saints."* —Paul, *Philemon 7* (NIV)

**TIP** – If you are afraid no one will talk, provide an activity to do together. My mom invited the women into the kitchen to help; my dad always offered a game of Ping Pong or a card game.

**TIP** – Ask an older child to have a game ready to play with any younger guests. He or she will feel useful, and it gives the parents an opportunity to visit together. Along those same lines, it's helpful to have a basket or drawer full of toys ready for any younger guests. I've saved our wooden blocks and a marble run for just such times.

**TIP**—The loneliest place to be is often in a crowd. To help out the new person in a large group, invite someone you know who is a "people lover" (an extrovert), and introduce him or her to the new, quieter guest. You can be assured that your new friend will not feel left out and will receive the needed attention.

**TIP** - Awkward silences around the table can be avoided if you have a couple of key questions in mind after the food has been passed. Fun and interesting ones I've tried are: "How did your husband propose?" and "How did you choose your current profession?" In celebrating my dad's eighty-fifth birthday, my brother Hyatt interviewed him with some key questions, which led to more reminiscing all around. One pertinent question he asked Dad, which you could ask any senior guest, was: "What do you consider your greatest achievement?" Funny enough, Dad said that besides fathering his great kids, it was the time he put together their first TV all by himself! Of course we all laughed when he recalled that, at first, the picture was upside down! If you're not sure how to introduce the question time, simply clink your glass with your fork, ask for everyone's attention and say something about how, in the interest of getting beyond the topic of the weather, and to know each other better, you would like to ask a question. Make the first question as non-threatening as possible—just one step beyond the weather, perhaps, so that guests remain at ease and good humor is maintained. In general, when you show genuine interest in another person, she or he is complimented and will return the interest.

**TIP** – Use questions beginning with the word "How" rather than "Why." It's less threatening, more friendly and open-ended, and it offers more information, which can then lead to further conversation. Much time can be wasted on just learning the answers to "What" questions, although they have their place. A good opening is: "Tell me about . . ." For example: "Tell me about the town you grew up in . . . tell our children about your first job . . . tell us about your trip to Africa . . ." Even the most reticent guest will open up with such friendly questions. Showing interest in another person is a genteel form of love, and that's what hospitality is all about.

**TIP** – Teach your own children conversation skills so they can interact with adults. I ask our girls to think of one or two questions to ask our guests. They have fun thinking of what to ask, and the table can become quite lively. Mary Grace may ask: "What's your favorite color?" Bethany asked recently: "Why did you become a pastor?" and Bonnie asked, "Why did you go to Biola University?" (I haven't taught them the "How" concept yet!) Each answer led to more dialogue, which was not only intriguing, but helpful to our girls. And, best of all, relationships between different ages was begun.

**TIP** - When celebrating an event in a guest's life—birthday, graduation, and so on—take the opportunity to verbally celebrate the person. Have someone jot down what everyone says and present the list as a gift to the honoree. You can let the other guests know in advance that you will be asking them to share, or "plant" a few among the crowd. You can be more spontaneous and tell everyone before the meal that during dessert, you will allow people to share what they admire about the special guest. My brother Hyatt is wonderful at leading these kinds of celebrations. He takes us all into the living room, makes a short speech about one of his guests— usually one of his family members—and then opens it up for everyone else. His point is this: "If you don't create the opportunity, people will go away from a nice gathering with a feeling that it was 'nice'—that's all, perhaps. But if you intentionally provide the opportunity for celebration, everyone gets blessed!"

**TIP** – Make the food preparation the activity. This can be fun for young and old alike. Place the ingredients and tools in different areas of the kitchen or dining table, leave out directions, and divide up your groups. Flour up to the elbows from making cookies, or doughnuts, is always good for close conversation.

Making personal pizzas or preparing a variety of Chinese food entrées can also be creative and entertaining. You can create "musical work stations" if you want a louder party: when the music changes, one work team moves to the next station. This idea takes some prepping work for the host, but you never have a dull moment once everyone arrives. Cleaning up together can be part of the evening as well—one person calls it her "patented 10-minute cleanup." She assigns the jobs, turns on some fast music, sets the timer for 10 minutes, and they all quit when the bell rings—both helpful and fun!

**TIP** – I don't always feel creative, but I know creative people, and so do you. Ask a creative friend to showcase his or her specialty at a friendly gathering. Find out what your friend will need to make his world-famous chili, and you provide what you can to make it happen. My sister-in-law Karen is a whiz at original card stamping, and she enjoys sharing her expertise and supplies. If I invite the guests, and make coffee and cookies, Karen brings the stamps and art paper, and the party is ready-made. In addition, everyone goes home with something they can use—a uniquely created homemade greeting card. Other ideas: Before the holidays, ask someone you know to show your friends how to wrap gifts or make bows, or another friend may be willing to demonstrate simple cake decorating or how to make yeast breads. The activity is the means for the fellowship, and friendships are built or strengthened.

**TIP** – Invite people you've wanted to introduce to each other. They may end up becoming best friends! Choose groups on the basis of one or more common interests. For example, two sets of friends may have kids with the same ages or they were originally from the Midwest. Others may have similar vocational or hobby interests. Two families who are both in the middle of a remodeling project may have different areas of expertise they could enjoy sharing with one another.

Once that connection is made, conversation flows easily, and relationships take off on their own. Your goal is to provide the setting where the friendships begin.

TIP – To make sure new people get acquainted with one another, pair people with someone they don't know or barely know, and provide a short list of questions. They can "interview" each other during dinner for about 20 minutes, and then introduce their partner to the rest of the group. This idea gets people to talk with one another, and it gives them something to talk about. And more people get to know each other all at once. There are always lots of laughter and common discoveries in the end.

TIP – Write descriptions of each of your guests and place them around the table with no name. Everyone circles the table to quietly read each description and then tries to guess their own. In the meantime, they've learned a lot about the other people there, and the table conversation has received a fun jumpstart.

TIP – Providing a "theme" for the night can be a great way to break the ice and get the party going. (see Chapter 9 for 25 theme ideas). My brother Steve, a former youth pastor, hosted "3 P's Parties" (pizza, Pepsi, and Ping Pong) to get acquainted with the kids in his youth group. He and his wife, Karen, invited a few kids over at a time, and they knew the menu and the main activity before they even arrived. It was simple to prepare and fun to anticipate. You wouldn't need to use alliteration to decide your menu and activity, but find a combination that works for you and is simple to carry out. (Actually, "carry-out" is also a good idea at times—that could be your "theme"— everyone brings their favorite fast food to share, and you provide the paper plates and ice cream!)

TIP –You might feel more relaxed about hospitality when you schedule an intentional activity. But, whatever you plan, give it to God and let Him run the evening. The results are His, and as you look back, you can find His touch even though things turned out in a completely different way than your original expectations. You can be assured it was just what He intended, and that's what matters.

## Preparing Your Heart and Mind

*Doors will open when we invite people in, not to take a tour but to share each other's hearts.* -—Georg Andersen, *Silent Witness: The Language of Your Home*

**TIP** - Practice hospitality. Do it over and over. The more you do it, the easier it is. Eventually, you won't be nervous, and you may even begin to enjoy it!

**TIP** - Ask a friend to practice with you. My mom and my aunt switched off Sunday dinners—one week at our house with baked chicken and rice, and the next week at Aunt Joy's with roast beef and potatoes. They "potlucked" the rest. Along the way they gained confidence and invited guests.

**TIP** - Invite a close friend over along with a new acquaintance. Your old friend can help with the conversation while you finish any last-minute preparations. Everyone benefits: Your guest makes two friends, and you are more relaxed in your host role.

**TIP** - If you think hospitality has to be a big deal, you won't do it. So change your mindset, and serve ice cream and chocolate sauce. No one ever complains about ice cream.

**TIP** – Since the definition of hospitality has to do with extending yourself for a "stranger," think of someone you've just met or someone who cannot return the favor, and invite them for dinner. Everyone is cliquish by nature. Step out of your clique on occasion, because Jesus stepped out of heaven for us. "Collect" people who may not have anyone else.

**TIP** – Hospitality needs to be fun and joy-filled or you won't want to do it again (and again.) It's too much work without the joy factor. What are the fun ingredients for you and your family? Think of an enjoyable time you had at someone else's house. Brainstorm with your kids and spouse about it. Was there something you could incorporate (or borrow) to increase the fun quotient at your next get-together? (A game? A recipe? A table? Tiki torches? Uncle Steve?) Your friend won't mind as long as you lend your croquet set for their next family reunion.

**TIP** – I can get overly anxious and stressed before guests arrive. That shows I'm focusing more on myself than the guests. (It may also mean I left too much to do at the last minute.) Last-minute meltdowns can indicate self-reliance vs. God-reliance. I need to remind myself: I'm doing this for God and by His strength for the sake of another.

**TIP** – Give each day to the Lord. One friend said, "God brings people to our house. At any given night, I may look back over the day and marvel at who He brought our way." She has an open home created by an open heart that looks a lot like heaven's hospitality.

**TIP** - Elaborate plans can be His will at particular events, as long as they are not solely done to demonstrate your personal expertise. Ask yourself: "Am I spending all this time to prepare so that others will think I'm wonderful?" or "Am I spending this time to make things as beautiful and comfortable as I can for my guests while still not getting crabby?"

**TIP** – If necessary, give yourself a pep talk before the company arrives: "It's not about my house, it's not about my food. It's just important that they come, they eat, that the kids play and make a big mess!" I always like the reminder: "People are coming to see me, not my house."

**TIP** – Welcome any mistakes that happen. If your guests only experience perfection in your home, they won't want to ask you to theirs. When you are comfortable with yourself, not some pretend-self or wish-you-were-self, you allow others to be the same. Less-than-perfect standards are a gift we give to others—unconsciously, perhaps—because we are saying: "I'm not perfect, so you don't need to pretend that you are." Mutuality at its best.

**TIP** – If you feel that you can't invite someone over because you are too busy and too tired, take a good look at your lifestyle and ask God some hard questions: "Lord, am I too busy?" "What would You want me to change so that our home could be more welcoming?" "How do You want me to go about making Your priorities lived out in my real life right now?" Write down your answers to any of the questions, and then ask a friend and the Lord to help you make any needed changes.

**TIP** – The same God who calls the woman with an elaborate mansion to be hospitable is the same God who asks the man renting a studio apartment to welcome others. Our homes look different, and our gifts and abilities are diverse. But God and His strength remain constant. If you are hesitant to invite someone over, examine your view of God rather than the size of your living room. Everyone who has a home can invite someone into it, even for just an hour and serving only a glass of iced tea.

**TIP** – Hospitality is for every Christian. Your attitude needs to be: "I'm doing it for the Lord. This is His work. This is His party." Your heart needs to be in the right place when you open your front door.

**TIP** – God's welcome to others looks different in every home. Allie puts out as much food as possible. She commented, "I figure the more food I put out, the less people will care about whether or not I have a centerpiece." DeDe likes simple votive candles strewn down the center of her table and white linen napkins pulled through ready-made raffia bows she keeps stored on an empty paper towel roll. (She invested in 15 votive candleholders, which she keeps for company occasions.) The setting of the welcome—how it looks—doesn't matter. Our job, and our joy, is to sit at God's table, experience His welcome for ourselves, and pass it on.

You get the theme here of prayer and fun. Bathe your heart and mind in prayer, and you will bless others, give God joy, and be blessed yourself. If any one of these ideas appealed to you, try it out today.

Remember the steps in Chapter 5: Start simply, start small, start in your own style, start as a servant. The important thing is to start. Happy hosting!

~~

# Anne's Coleslaw

Shredded cabbage (I added broccoli slaw as well)

Dried cranberries

Blue cheese (I used Feta cheese)

Cilantro (I forgot)

Peanuts

Paul Newman or Trader Joe's Ginger Sesame Salad Dressing to taste

Yum—so crunchy and colorful—any time of day, and as you can see—EASY!

# Chapter 8

# Food for Body and Soul

Joanne and Carole noticed that their single friend, Lisa, never had anyone over. One day they both said to her, "Lisa, we want to come for dinner. We need a break from cooking for our families, and we want to spend some time with you at your house."

Lisa, more than a little startled, stammered, "I wouldn't know what to cook. It would have to come out of a can."

"That's fine with us," they enthused, and to dinner they came. It came out of a can.

A couple months later, they did it again. "Lisa, it's time we come over." This time it was a little more than a canned meal, and a whole lot of fun besides. Eventually, Lisa began to do the inviting. She learned that friendship, not food, was the important thing. And practicing hospitality with a couple of close (and bold) friends helped her become at ease with inviting and serving in her home. (There is a cookbook titled, *The Can-Opener Gourmet* . . . perhaps Lisa could be a contributing editor for Volume 2 . . .)

While the question, "What's for dinner?" may be the easiest one you have to consider on any given day, you might feel stumped when it comes to making a company meal. And it may be the main reason you haven't begun practicing hospitality.

"If I ask someone over, what in the world will I serve?"

One uncertainty leads to another: "What kind of meal should I make?" "How much do I prepare?" "Do I have to go to the store?" "If so, when?" "And when will I cook?" ("And how will I cook it? Oh, that's right, I don't cook, so that settles it!")

For some, meal-planning anxiety stops the invitation before it's given. It's too hard, too much to think about. Therefore, it's out of the question.

While food can be foremost in our mind when we think of hospitality, what's on the plate is not the main event. (If necessary, read that sentence again.) Food just accompanies the main event: God's welcome and ours. That's why this recipe chapter is toward the end of the book. It's not the most important thing. What you serve is a "side dish" to friendship and community. But side dishes are fun and often delicious. They complement the entrée. They enhance the enjoyment of being together.

With that in mind, recipes are included here to allow a host and hostess to concentrate on what is the focus—the guests. Entrées listed aren't divided into breakfast, lunch or dinner since many can be interchanged. Chocolate, coffee times and leftovers will get their own special categories, although chocolate for dinner is an option for some!

The chapter concludes with a "Pantry List"—recommended items to keep on hand to make hospitality easier and more spontaneous.

Here's the point: there is no category for "Company Meals." Anything you prepare can be for company. People are just happy to be invited. They love it that you thought of them and that they, after all, didn't have to do the cooking. Hospitality is about people, and food is the side attraction. All the recipes listed below are company fare, the same as your favorite egg scramble or taco salad. Open the can, cook it with love and an inviting heart, and your guests will love you. And best of all, they will know that God loves them.

# Food You Can Make Ahead

Organization is the key to being relaxed and ready for your company. Anything you can do the night before, or the day before, or even a week ahead, can be just what you needed to make your company evening run smoothly. Here are some delicious do-ahead ideas.

### Chicken Reuben

### (Serve with baked potatoes and green salad)

1 - boned/skinned chicken breast per person

1-16 oz. can sauerkraut, drained

½ lb. Swiss or Jack cheese, grated

1 bottle Thousand Island dressing

Layer in 9x13 pan: chicken, sauerkraut, and cheese to cover. Pour dressing over chicken. Cover with foil and refrigerate until baking. Bake at 350° for 1 hour.

## Hearty Enchilada Casserole

## (Serve with cornbread or warmed corn tortillas)

2 lbs. hamburger or ground turkey, browned with 1 onion, chopped; drain. One 7 oz. can green chilies, 2 – 10 ½ oz. cans enchilada sauce; 2 cans cream of mushroom soup, 2 small cans of sliced olives, 12 corn tortillas. 2 cups shredded cheddar cheese. Add sauce to hamburger and simmer 10 minutes. Mix chilies with soup and heat. Add to meat mixture. Tear half tortillas and line bottom of 9x13 pan. Cover with a layer of meat/sauce, a layer of cheese, and repeat. Let stand for 30 minutes or overnight in refrigerator. Bake 30-40 minutes at 350°. I've also layered this in a crock pot before church— done by lunch.

## Daria's Overnight Luscious French Toast

## (A great entrée to make for holiday breakfasts; serve with sausage on the side.)

Mix and pour into 15x10x1" pan (jelly roll pan): ½ cup butter, melted; ½ cup honey; 2 t. cinnamon.

Stir together: 6 eggs, 1 cup milk, ½ cup - 1 cup orange juice, 1 T. vanilla, ½ t. salt, ½ t. cinnamon, 2 t. orange zest (opt.), ½ cup sugar.

Slice French bread loaf into 16 slices, dip in egg mixture, arrange in pan. Pour remaining mixture over bread. Cover and refrigerate at least one hour, or overnight. Bake at 400°– 425° for 15 minutes until puffed. Turn bread over before serving. Spread gooey sauce over and sprinkle with powdered sugar. No need for syrup!

Opt: Orange Honey Butter: ½ cup butter, ¼ cup honey, and 1 t. grated orange peel.

## Morning Egg Bake

**(Make on Saturday, serve after church on Sunday with sliced fruit and blueberry muffins. If teenagers are included, add a side of hash browns.)**

10 – 12 slices toasted, cubed bread

1 lb. Sausage, browned and drained.

Mix 2 cups cheddar cheese, grated; 4 eggs, beaten and 2 ½ cups milk, and ¾ t. dry mustard.

Layer bread and sausage. Pour liquid mixture over. Cover and refrigerate overnight.

Mix ½ cup milk and 1 can cream of mushroom soup together and pour over the top. Bake at 350° for 1 ½ hours. (Use time-bake on your oven if available and you will be gone while cooking.)

## Trishie's Chili Chicken Tortilla Casserole

**(Serve with cornbread or Spanish rice and green salad; great use of leftover chicken or turkey.)**

Lay 3 cooked and diced chicken breasts (about 3-4 cups) on bottom of 9x13 pan. Sprinkle with ½ cup onion, salt and pepper. Cover with 8-12 cut-up corn tortillas.

Mix together and add to layers: 2 cans cream soups, 1 can green chili salsa (or 1 cup of any salsa), ½ cup chicken broth, 1 large can chili beans. Place 2-3 cups grated cheese on top. Bake 40-45 minutes at 350°. Remove 15 minutes before eating.

## Rice Sausage Brunch Bake

**(Serve with hot fruit casserole and biscuits; easy to double for two 9x13s.)**

1 lb. bulk sausage

4 ½ cup water

2 packages dry chicken noodle soup

1 cup celery (diced)

1 medium onion (chopped)

½ green or red pepper (chopped, opt.)

1 small can mushrooms

1 cup uncooked rice

In large skillet or Dutch oven, brown sausage, drain. Heat water to boiling, pour into sausage and stir. Mix in soup mixes, bring to a boil and remove from heat. Add remaining ingredients. Put in 9x13 pan and cover. May refrigerate overnight or bake immediately at 300° for 1 hour, 15 minutes, or until liquid is absorbed.

# Food That Cooks All Day

Actually, most of the following dishes cook just half a day, but they all make the house smell wonderful, and most of the work is done early in the day. Your last-minute time can be spent making a salad, heating rolls, and vacuuming under the table (or not . . .)

## French Dip Beef Sandwiches

### (Serve with coleslaw and rice pilaf)

¼ cup olive oil

1 5-lb. chuck roast, fat trimmed

2 large garlic cloves, minced

salt and pepper

1 cup beef broth

1 cup freshly-brewed strong coffee

1 cup red wine

1 package dry onion soup mix

1 cup water

8 sandwich-sized French rolls

Rub roast with garlic and seasonings. Brown in oil in large stockpot. Drain oil, add the next 5 ingredients, cover and simmer approximately 4 hours. Turn once during cooking. Heat rolls at 250°, slice roast and make sandwiches. Serve broth on the side for dipping. This is a family favorite.

## Split Pea Soup

### (Serve with French rolls or crackers)

In a crock pot, combine:

1-16 ounce bag split peas, rinsed, drained and picked over

3 stalks celery

chopped

3 large carrots

chopped

2 cups chicken broth

4 cups water

3 slices Canadian bacon or leftover ham, chopped (optional)

1 teaspoon salt

Cover and cook on high for 4-5 hours until peas are tender and soup is smooth when stirred.

## Smoked Sausage Pot

### (Serve with biscuits and fresh fruit)

1 package smoked sausage, sliced and browned

1 large onion, sliced

6 medium potatoes, quartered

2 cans green beans (canned beans work better than fresh because of the juices needed for the potatoes)

dash of pepper

1 glove garlic

Place all ingredients in crock pot in the morning and forget it. Delicious all-in-one dinner.

## Tri-tip and Salsa

### (Serve with medium flour tortillas, shredded cheese, sour cream and chopped onions. Melts in your mouth.)

Place beef or pork tri-tip in crock pot. Add large can black beans and medium jar salsa or canned tomatoes with green chilies. Cook on low all day. Makes shredded beef or pork tacos.

## Sweet and Sour Brisket of Beef

### (Delicious served with mashed potatoes.
### The sauce makes the gravy.)

1 beef brisket, 4-5 lbs.

¼ cup flour

1 packet of dry onion soup mix

1 can tomato soup

¼ t. black pepper

2 T. brown sugar

2 T. red wine vinegar

Dredge brisket in flour, shake excess, and place in crock-pot. Combine soups, pepper and ¼ cup water in small bowl, stir and pour mixture over brisket. Cover and cook on high 6 hours. Remove brisket and keep warm. Strain liquid and spoon off fat. Heat in saucepan and add vinegar and brown sugar until sugar melts. Spoon enough sauce over beef to moisten, and serve the remaining sauce on the side.

## Easy Party Chicken for Tired Homemakers

**(The apricot preserves give this a tropical flair, so serve with steamed rice and a green vegetable.)**

1 fryer, cut-up and skinned

1 package dry onion soup

1 cup Thousand Island dressing

12 oz. apricot preserves (optional: orange marmalade or apricot-pineapple preserves)

Place chicken in greased casserole. Sprinkle soup mix evenly over top, then pour dressing over all. Place several spoonfuls of preserves over chicken. Cover and bake at 350° for 1 ½ hours.

# Food to Feed a Crowd

It doesn't have to cost a week's salary to serve a lot of people. Cooking from scratch saves money and often tastes better. Buying convenience foods saves time and effort.

## Taco Soup I (Beef)

**(Both taco soups can be served with sides of sour cream, shredded cheese, olives, cilantro, and tortilla chips.)**

¼ lb. ground beef

1 small onion, diced

1 -16 oz. can tomatoes

1- 8 oz. can tomato sauce

1-16 oz. can kidney beans

½ package taco seasoning

Brown beef and onion together and drain. Blend tomatoes in blender until smooth. Add to beef mixture and add remaining ingredients. Simmer 20 minutes and ladle into bowls filled with a few tortilla chips, and preferred toppings on the side.

## Taco Soup II (Chicken)

**(Both soups double or triple easily and are relatively inexpensive yet appeal to all ages. Keep the spicy salsa on the side for the braver guests, and the kids will be happier. Good served with cornbread and extra chips.)**

2- 14 oz. cans chicken broth

1 ½ to 2 cups diced, cooked chicken

1 medium onion, chopped

1- 4 oz. can chopped green chilies

1 T. chili powder

1 can whole kernel corn (opt.)

2 cups broken tortilla chips; shredded cheddar cheese

## Four Bean Chicken Chili

**(This makes a lot! Make it as spicy as you like and use any leftover meat or chicken. Serve with cornbread or breadsticks.)**

4 - 15 oz. cans beans of your choice (black, pinto, white and/or kidney with liquid)

3 - 15 oz. cans chopped tomatoes (may use Mexican style for more zip)

1 ½ cups shredded cooked chicken, pork, or beef)

1 t. Cumin

1 bay leaf

½ t. hot pepper sauce or red pepper flakes (opt.)

Mix all ingredients into large stock pot and heat over medium high heat. Bring to a boil, then reduce heat, cover, and simmer for 30 minutes, stirring occasionally. Discard bay leaf before serving. This chili freezes well up to three months.

## Tammy's Oven BBQ Chicken

**(Adjust the spice to suit your guests; for a crowd, cook two different batches— one spicy, one mild. Serve with oven fried potatoes or steamed rice.)**

5 lbs. chicken pieces

Cover with the following sauce: 2 cups ketchup, 2 cups BBQ sauce, ¼ cup Worcestershire sauce, 3 T. brown sugar, 4 T. soy sauce, 2 t. crushed red pepper (opt.), 1 can drained crushed pineapple. Bake uncovered at 400° for 1 hour. Easier cleanup if you line your pan with foil.

# Corn Sausage Chowder

## (Delicious served with cornbread or rolls.)

1 lb. smoked sausage

1 large onion

2 large potatoes, peeled and diced

2 t. salt

1 t. basil

1 T. dried parsley

½ t. pepper

2 cups water

1 can creamed corn

1 can whole kernel corn

1 large can evaporated milk

Cut sausage and brown in Dutch oven. Add onion and sauté until soft. Stir in potatoes, salt, basil, pepper, parsley, and water. Cover and simmer 15 minutes. Stir in corn with liquid, milk and water. Cover. Heat to just boiling and serve. Easy to double.

# Food to Fit the Budget

When you see things on a great sale, it's good to stock up and keep the items in the freezer for when company calls, whether it's boneless chuck roast or a turkey breast. I like to make a roast for Sunday dinner and bag up the leftovers for burritos, fajitas or a favorite Mexican casserole or soup later on. Homemade soups are inexpensive and special for this generation raised on fast food.

### Make-the-House-a-Heaven–Pot Roast

**(Savory aromas fill your home with this inexpensive yet delicious stew. Serve with biscuits and sautéed apples.)**

3-4 lb. boneless chuck roast

1 can cream of mushroom soup

1 pouch dry onion soup

1 ¼ cup water

6 medium potatoes, quartered

6 carrots, cut into 2" pieces

2 T. flour

Brown roast in oil in Dutch oven or large skillet. Spoon off fat. Stir in soup, soup mix, and 1 cup water. Cover and cook on simmer 2 hours. Add vegetables and cook 45 minutes. Remove roast and vegetables, keep warm.

Mix flour and remaining ¼ cup water until smooth. Add to soup mixtures and boil until thickening.

## Crab Giovanni

**(I always use imitation crab but the original recipe calls for fresh or canned. Serve with French bread and green salad.)**

¼ cup butter or margarine

1 medium onion, chopped

¼ lb. mushrooms, sliced

1 clove garlic, minced

6 oz. shell pasta, cooked to al dente

¾ lb. cooked crab

¼ cup sliced green or black olives

1 cup cheddar cheese, grated

¼ cup sour cream

1 15 oz. can diced tomatoes

¾ t. salt

½ t. dry basil

Sauté onions, mushrooms, and garlic in butter about 5 minutes and combine with cooked and drained pasta. Add crab, olives, cheese, sour cream, tomatoes and their liquid, salt and basil. Pour mixture into a greased 1 ½ quart baking dish. Bake, uncovered for 30 minutes at 350° until bubbly. May make ahead and bake the next day.

## Moo Shu What-You-Have

**(You can use 1 pork chop, a cup of leftover roast, or a chicken breast instead of the beef round tip steak for this quick and tasty Chinese dish. Serve with white or fried rice.)**

1 lb. beef round tip steak

2 T. soy sauce

2 T. water

3 cups packaged coleslaw mix

1 T. sesame oil

⅔ cup slice green onions

1 t. cornstarch, dissolved in ¼ cup water

2 garlic cloves, crushed

8 medium flour tortillas, warmed

2 t. sugar

⅓ cup hoisin sauce (kids may prefer plum sauce)

Cut steak into thin strips. Combine soy sauce and water, add beef, tossing to coat. Cover and marinate in refrigerator 20 minutes. Remove beef and discard marinade. Heat large skillet over medium-high heat until hot. Add beef and stir-fry 1 to 2 minutes. Add coleslaw mix, green onion and cornstarch mixture. Cook and stir until sauce is thickened. To assemble, spread one side of tortilla with 2 t. hoisin or plum sauce. Spoon ½ cup beef mixture in center of each tortilla. Fold bottom edge up over filling and overlap edges like a burrito.

## Sweet and Sour What-You-Have

## (Serve with steamed or fried rice and egg rolls.)

2 T. oil

1 lb. boneless pork or chicken (or leftover meat)

1 can pineapple chunks

½ cup dark corn syrup

¼ cup vinegar

2 T. catsup

2 T. soy sauce

1 clove garlic, minced

2 T. corn starch

½ cup green pepper, chunked

Brown meat of choice. Add pineapple with juice, corn syrup, vinegar, catsup, soy sauce, and garlic. Bring to a boil, simmer 10 minutes. Mix corn starch and 2 T. water and add mixture and green pepper to pan. Boil 2 minutes, until thickened, stirring constantly. Serve over rice.

# Pork (or Chicken) Satay

## (Use as a main dish over rice or as an appetizer. Serve with spinach salad.)

1 ½ lbs. pork tenderloin or chicken breasts

¼ cup butter

1 T. lemon juice

grated lemon rind from 1 lemon

½ t. Tabasco sauce (opt.)

3 T. grated onion

3 T. light brown sugar

1 t. coriander

½ t. ground cumin

¼ t. ground ginger

1 clove crushed garlic

½ cup soy sauce or teriyaki sauce

salt and pepper to taste

Cut the meat into ¾ inch cubes and place in a shallow glass dish. Melt the butter in a saucepan and add the remaining ingredients. Bring to a boil and simmer 5 minutes. Pour over the meat, cover and leave ½ hour to overnight in the refrigerator. Remove meat from the marinade (reserve), and put 5 or 6 pieces on a skewer. Grill on a barbeque for 15 minutes until done, turning frequently. The meat may also be cooked in a broiler. Reheat the marinade and pour over the meat. Set the skewers on a platter in a bed of rice. Good served with peanut dipping sauce.

## Hot Bread Reubens

**(Use your dough cycle of bread machine or frozen bread loaves to make this easier to prepare. Good use of leftover Easter ham. Serve with coleslaw.)**

1 loaf of raw bread dough

¼ cup Thousand Island dressing

6 oz. sliced ham or corned beef

4 oz. sliced Swiss or Jack cheese

1- 8 oz. can sauerkraut, drained

1 egg, beaten

caraway seeds (optional)

On greased sheet, roll dough into rectangle. Down the middle of the dough, top with layers of meat, cheese, sauerkraut, and dressing. Make cuts 1 inch apart on both sides of the filling. Alternating sides, fold the strips of dough at an angle across filling. Cover and let rise 15 minutes. Brush with egg white and sprinkle seeds. Bake at 400° for 25 minutes.

## Meatball Soup (or Hamburger Soup)

**(My mother served 50 college students with this hearty but inexpensive soup. If you make the meatballs ahead, or buy frozen, it's easy to put together at the last minute.)**

Brown meatballs (or you can use 1 lb. of hamburger, crumbled and drained.) Place in large pot with 2 cups water; 2-3 potatoes, diced; 2-3 carrots, cut in ½ inch slices; 2-3 stalks celery sliced, 1 large onion, sliced; 1 - 8 oz. can tomato sauce, 1 - 15 oz. can tomatoes; salt and pepper to taste; ¼ t. garlic powder; ½ t. Italian seasoning. Combine and add enough water to make amount of soup desired. More veggies and tomato sauce may be added to increase quantity. Simmer one hour or longer to enhance flavors. Add ½ head of cabbage the last 15 minutes.

# Food to Fix Last Minute

Spontaneity flourishes when you know you can whip up a yummy meal in minutes. When someone new comes to town, or your manicurist gets dumped by her boyfriend and need her spirits lifted, a quick invitation to dinner may be just what is needed. A quick meal is easier for everyone and can taste just as good.

## Chicken Piccata

**(This is especially quick if you pound the chicken before freezing. Serve with baked potatoes or barley.)**

Pound boneless, skinless chicken breast until ½" thick. Dredge in flour. Melt butter in skillet and sauté until browned, approximately 5 minutes per side. Sprinkle seasoned salt or Herbes de Provence and lemon juice while cooking. Remove to platter and garnish with lemon slices.

## Katy's Chicken Supreme

**(If you keep the boneless, skinless chicken breasts on hand in your freezer, you can make this delicious recipe in a flash. Just add rice or pasta and a salad.)**

Season chicken breasts and pour over equal parts of cream of mushroom soup and sour cream. Sprinkle with paprika (for color.) Cover pan and bake 45–50 minutes at 350°.

## Beef with Pea Pods

**(To double recipe, double all but meat. Delicious and easy to do even after arriving home after a long day. Serve with white or brown rice and 5 –cup salad.)**

1 lb. steak , cut in 4" slices.

Sauce:

2 t. cornstarch

½ t. salt

¼ cup water

1 t. sugar

⅛ t. pepper

2 T. soy sauce

(Blend and set aside)

2 T. oil

1 clove garlic, minced

½ t. grated ginger root

6 oz. pea pods

4 oz. water chestnuts

Preheat wok or large skillet. Add oil. Stir–fry garlic and ginger root 30 seconds. Add peas and chestnuts, fry 1 minute. Remove peas and chestnuts. Add more oil if necessary. Add beef, fry 2-3 minutes until browned. Stir in sauce, cooking till bubbly. Add peas and chestnuts.

## Sopa de Fideo

### (Almost a meal in one pot, just add a green or fruit salad on the side with French bread.)

1 lb. hamburger

12 oz. fideo noodles or thin spaghetti, broken up

½ lb. cheddar

2 T. oil

1 onion

1 medium can whole tomatoes

1 ½ cups boiling water

1 green pepper, diced

1 – 2 stalks celery, diced

1 medium can whole kernel corn

1 T. salt

1 t. pepper

1 ¼ t. chili powder

Break raw pasta into small pieces (I use hammer while it's still in the package.) Brown pasta in oil. Remove and brown beef and drain. Return pasta to skillet and add remaining ingredients except the cheese. Simmer 20 minutes until pasta is tender. Sprinkle cheese on top and add lid to melt. Serve immediately. Feeds a crowd quickly.

## Chicken Caesar Wraps

## (Makes 4, kids may prefer the wrap without the dressing)

Marinade 1 lb. boneless, skinless chicken breasts in 1 t. crushed garlic, 1 t. lemon pepper; ½ t. Italian seasoning, and 3 T. olive oil for 20 minutes. Grill or broil chicken for 10 – 14 minutes. Remove and cut into strips.

In a small bowl, combine dressing: 1 cup sour cream, 2 T. milk, 3 T. Parmesan cheese, ½ t. Italian seasoning (or Lemon pepper), ½ t. crushed garlic.

Place chopped Romaine lettuce and sliced chicken in warm flour tortilla. Top with dressing and fold.

## Spaghetti Carbonara

**(I've tried several variations of this recipe and this is the easiest and the tastiest. Good use of leftover Easter ham. When I buy bacon, I'll fry up extra pieces and freeze to add to this yummy entrée.)**

8 oz. cooked spaghetti, keep hot, drain. Brown ½ lb. diced bacon, remove fat. Add ½ cup oil. Sauté ½ diced onion and ¼ lb. ham, sliced in strips. Add ¼ cup butter, ½ cup chicken broth. Remove from heat. Add 2 beaten eggs, stir to cook. Mix in ¼ cup parsley. Sprinkle 1 cup mozzarella cheese or ½ cup mozzarella and ½ cup parmesan cheese. Serve with garlic bread and sliced fruit.

# Easy Desserts

Dessert is not for every night, but when company's coming, it's fun to end a good meal with something sweet. Here are some simple but delicious treats to please your palate and those you love.

## Nutmeg Pound Cake

1 yellow cake mix

1 small vanilla instant pudding

4 eggs

¾ cup sherry or less

1 T. nutmeg

¾ cup oil

Mix and pour into bundt pan, 9x13 or two loaf pans. Bake 350° for 40 – 50 minutes. Sprinkle with powdered sugar.

## Lemon Cake Pie

**(So easy if you have the pie crust ready in the freezer—see "Homemade Freezer Pie Crusts.")**

1 - 9" pastry shell

2 eggs, separated

1 to 2 T. grated lemon peel

½ cup lemon juice

1 cup mild

1 cup sugar

¼ cup flour

¼ t. salt

Heat oven to 350°. Prepare pastry. Beat egg whites until stiff peaks form. Beat egg yolks. Add lemon peel, juice and milk, and beat. Add sugar, flour and salt and beat until smooth. Fold into egg whites. Pour into pastry-lined pie pan. Bake 45-50 minutes. Serve warm or cool. Top with Cool Whip or whipped cream, if desired. (see Easy As Pie Vinegar Pie Crust end of Chapter 1)

## Apple Bread Pudding

4 slices bread

toasted and cubed

¾ cup hot milk

2 T. butter

2 eggs, beaten

dash salt

⅓ cup sugar

¼ t. each cinnamon and nutmeg

½ cup raisins

1 apple, pared and dice

¼ cup brown sugar

Arrange bread cubes in buttered casserole. Cover with milk and dots of butter. Let bread soak for 20 minutes. Add remaining ingredients except brown sugar and blend with bread. Sprinkle brown sugar over top. Bake at 300° for 40 minutes. Makes 4 servings.

## Ice Cream Sandwiches

Place a scoop of ice scream between two large chocolate chip cookies. Roll sides in chopped nuts or sprinkles. Wrap in waxed paper and freeze for about 30 minutes.

## Peanut Butter Pie

1-8oz. softened cream cheese

1 cup powdered sugar

1–12 oz. Cool Whip

½ cup to 1 cup peanut butter

¼ cup milk (optional)

Mix and pour into prepared graham cracker crust and refrigerate until served.

## Orange Pumpkin Cake

½ cup butter or margarine, softened

1 ¼ cup sugar

2 eggs

1 cup cooked or canned pumpkin

½ cup orange juice

1/4 cup milk

1 T. grated orange peel

2 cups flour

3 t. baking powder

1 t. cinnamon

½ t. baking soda

½ t. salt

½ teaspoon ground ginger

½ t. ground allspice

½ cup chopped nuts (opt.)

Cream butter and sugar. Add eggs, one a t a time. Add pumpkin, orange juice, milk and orange peel. Combine dry ingredients; add to creamed ingredients. Fold in nuts. Pour into 9x13 pan. Bake at 350° for 30 minutes.

Orange frosting: combine ⅓ cup butter or margarine, softened; 3 cups powdered sugar. Beat in 3 T. milk, 2 t. orange juice, and 4 t. grated orange peel. Spread on cooled cake and garnish with orange zest.

## Heritage Inn Apple Bread Pudding

**(This can easily be doubled or tripled for a group and is wonderful with maple glazed sausage. Use for Sunday brunch or Thanksgiving morning.)**

1 loaf of French or sourdough bread, cut into two inch pieces (day- old works well)

1 ½ cups milk

½ cup sugar

3 t. cinnamon

2 t. vanilla

1 t. almond extract

8 eggs, beaten

2 cups apples, diced (rhubarb is also wonderful!)

1 cup pecans, broken

½ butter, cut in pieces

Spread bread pieces in greased 9x13 pan. Sprinkle with nuts and apples. Mix all ingredients except brown sugar and butter. Pour over bread. Cover and refrigerate overnight. Before baking, add butter pieces. Sprinkle with brown sugar. Bake at 350° for 1 to 1 ½ hours. Serve with maple syrup.

# To Serve on the Side

When you have an extra person at the table, a simple side dish may be all that's needed to make the dinner stretch enough to satisfy. Keeping canned biscuits on hand or your bread machine at the ready is also a good last-minute crowd-pleaser.

### Sautéed Apples

5 medium Golden Delicious apples, peeled and thinly sliced

¼ cup butter or margarine

¼ cup water

½ cup sugar

½ t. ground cinnamon

In a large skillet, sauté apples in butter for one minute. Add water; bring to a boil. Sprinkle with sugar and cinnamon. Reduce heat; cover and simmer for 10-12 minutes or until apples are tender. A quick and unusual side dish, good with roast beef, pork chops, or an egg brunch casserole.

## Corn Pudding

1 can creamed corn

2 eggs

2 T. flour

2 t. sugar

1 t. salt

1 cup grated cheddar

Combine all ingredients and pour into well-buttered casserole. Bake 45 minutes at 350 degrees. Easy to double.

## French Style Rice

1 cube butter/margarine

1 clove garlic, minced

1 medium onion, chopped

1 t. parsley

1 cup raw rice

1 can beef broth

⅓ cup water

1 can mushrooms

Place all in casserole, cover and bake 45 minutes at 350 degrees.

## Hot Fruit Casserole

3 cans of drained fruit (peaches, pears, apricots); 1 jar of applesauce; butter; cinnamon.

Drain fruit. Layer fruit with applesauce, pats of butter, and cinnamon in between layers. Bake for 1 hour at 325°. May use crock pot.

## Rancho BBQ Beans

1 lb. dry pink or red beans

6 cups water, to cook the beans

½ lb. turkey smoked sausage

1 medium onion

chopped fine

2 cloves garlic, minced

¼ cup hot diced chili (more or less to taste preference)

⅓ cup molasses

⅓ cup ketchup

⅓ cup barbeque sauce

2 t. Worcestershire sauce

Sort and wash beans. Place the beans in a slow cooker (crock pot) with 6 cups of hot water. Cook on low for 8-10 hours (overnight). When the beans are cooked and tender, drain the water. Gently mix all the ingredients in the crockpot. Cook 3-6 hours before serving. Makes a great side dish for ham or hamburgers.

## Five Cup Salad

4 cups of fresh or canned fruit. Add 1 cup sour cream. (Coconut is optional). Stir and refrigerate for 30 minutes.

## Homemade Creamed Corn

20 oz. frozen corn

1 cup cream or half and half

1 cup milk

1 t. Salt

¼ t. accent or seasoned salt

2 T. sugar

pinch of pepper

2 T. melted butter

2 T. flour

Mix corn, cream, milk, sugar, and seasonings. Simmer 5 minutes. Add a mixture of melted butter and flour. Stir until thickened.

# To Serve for Afternoon Tea (or Morning Coffee)

My favorite kind of hospitality is serving girlfriends and their kids treats with coffee or tea. Here are some easy and delicious recipes that accompany fun and satisfying conversation around the table.

### Ceslie's Banana Cake

⅓ cup shortening

2 eggs

1 and 1/4 cup sugar

1 t. vanilla

1 t. baking powder

¾ t. baking soda

1 t. salt

1 and ½ cup flour

Add: 1 cup mashed bananas and 1/2 cup sour milk or buttermilk

Bake 30-35 min. 350°. May layer with sliced bananas and sliced almonds for something fancy on top of cream cheese frosting.

## Mama Marian's Scones

2 cups flour

1 T. baking powder

½ t. salt

¼ cup sugar

½ cup or so of dried cranberries, raisins, etc. (my etc. included mini-chocolate chips...)

1 ½ cups heavy whipping cream

Topping:

2 T. melted butter (that lasted for all 3 batches for me), or 2 T. sugar (raw, if you have it)

Preheat oven to 425° if cooking immediately. Combine all dry ingredients and mix in cream. Knead gently on floured board (hint: don't wear black jeans while making 3 batches...)Pat into circle and cut into wedges. Butter and sugar top and bake 15 minutes. Makes 8.

Directions for freezing:

Make scones as directed and place on cookie sheet. Freeze uncovered. When frozen put into freezer Ziploc bag. When ready to bake, place on lightly greased cookie sheet and bake at 375° for 15-18 minutes.

## Davia's Butterscotch Pumpkin Bread

1 cup butterscotch morsels

2 cups flour

1 ¾ cups sugar

1 T. baking powder

1 ½ t. ground cinnamon

1 t. salt

½ nutmeg

1 cup pumpkin

½ oil

3 eggs

1 t. vanilla

Melt morsels in microwave, 30 seconds at a time, stirring in between. Combine pumpkin, oil, eggs, vanilla and morsels. Add flour, sugar, baking powder, spices. Spoon batter into greased bundt or loaf pan. Bake 40-50 minutes at 350°. Cool in pan 15 minutes, remove and sprinkle with powdered sugar.

## Raspberry (or Apricot) Pastry

Mix with fork: 2 cups flour, 1 t. salt, 2 sticks butter.

Add: 1 cup sour cream and refrigerate overnight. In the morning, divide dough in half, roll into two 12 " rectangles, approximately ½" thick. Spread with raspberry or apricot jam. Sprinkle shredded coconut lightly and fold 3 times.

Bake on cookie sheet 45 minutes at 350°; let stand for 10 minutes. Sprinkle with powdered sugar and slice diagonally. Melts in your mouth!

## Irish Coffee Cake

Filling:

⅔ cup firmly packed brown sugar

1 T. butter or margarine, melted

1 cup chopped nuts

Cake:

1 yellow cake mix

1 cup sour cream

½ cup oil

4 eggs

Beat cake ingredients for 5 minutes. Fill bundt pan with half of mixture, then filling, followed by remaining batter. Use knife to swirl. Bake for 50 minutes at 350°.

## Chili Relleno Casserole

½ lb. Jack cheese

½ lb. Cheddar cheese

1 can whole green chilies (diced works fine)

½ cup Bisquick

1 egg

1 t. salt

1 ½ cup milk

Clean chilies of all seeds. Grate cheese. Layer grated cheese and chilies in buttered 9x9 dish. Top with cheese. Mix remaining ingredients and pour over top of cheese and chilies. Bake at 350° for 40 minutes.

# Chocolate

Of course, there are entire cookbooks on *chocolate*, so these are just a few to soothe the soul, increase endorphins and put the "happy" back in the camper.

## Laurie's Triple Chocolate Crock-Pot Cake

1 package chocolate cake mix

2 cups sour cream

1 small package instant chocolate pudding

1 cup chocolate chips

¾ cup oil

4 eggs

1 cup water

Mix in large bowl until smooth. Pour into crockpot, cook on low 6–8 hours. Serve in bowls with vanilla ice cream. Whipped cream and sprinkles are optional.

## DeDe's Deep Dark Chocolate Cake

2 cups sugar

1 ¾ cups flour

¾ cup dry cocoa

1 ½ t. baking powder

1 ½ t. baking soda

1 t. salt 2 eggs

½ cup oil

1 cup milk

2 t. vanilla

1 cup boiling water

Combine dry ingredients, add next 4 ingredients and beat 2 minutes. Stir in boiling water. Bake in 9x13 pan at 350° for 35-40 minutes. Cool and frost.

## Chocolate Town Pie

½ cup margarine or butter

2 beaten eggs

1 t. vanilla

1 cup sugar

½ cup flour

1 cup chocolate chips

1 cup nuts (opt.)

Mix and spoon into an unbaked pie shell. Bake at 350° for 45-50 minutes. Serve while warm with vanilla ice cream or whipped cream.

## Pot de Crème

¾ cup milk heated to boiling point. Place in blender or, use immersion blender, 1 cup semi-sweet chocolate chips, 1 egg, 1 t. vanilla and hot milk. Blend at low speed for one minute.

Place in small custard cups and bake approximately 20-30 minutes at 350°. Chill several hours. Serve with whipped cream, sprinkled w/ cinnamon.

## Bethany's Chocolate Sauce

⅓ cup water

¼ cup sugar

1 T. butter

¾ cup semi-sweet chocolate chips

½ t. vanilla

In a small saucepan, bring the water, sugar and butter to a gentle boil. Boil for 2 minutes. Remove from the heat; add the chocolate chips and vanilla. Whisk until chips are melted and mixture is smooth.

## Tollhouse Muffins

2 cups flour

⅓ cup sugar

½ t. salt

1 t. baking soda

2 t. baking powder

⅔ cup brown sugar

Combine and add: ½ cup milk, 1 cup sour cream or plain yogurt, ½ cup melted butter, 1 t. vanilla. Stir in 1 cup chocolate chips. Makes 18 muffins. Bake at 375° for 20 minutes.

# Food to Feed the Kids

Kids are kids, what can I say? One week they love broccoli, the next week they sneak it onto their sister's plate with an oh-so-innocent look. These recipes can't be guaranteed to be loved every week, but maybe one will turn out to be a family favorite. (Good luck!)

## Pepsi Chicken

**(Yes, you use Pepsi or any soda although grape doesn't have a great look to it; serve with steamed rice and broccoli.)**

1 cut-up fryer

Mix:

1 cup ketchup

1 cup Pepsi

1-2 T. Worcestershire sauce

Pour over chicken in skillet. Cover and simmer 45 minutes.

## Debbie's Western Chili Casserole

**(This fits every category—inexpensive, quick and appeals to all ages. Serve with salad and bread sticks.)**

1 lb. ground beef

½ cup chopped celery (opt.)

1 cup grated cheese

1 cup chopped onion

¼ t. pepper

2 cups crushed Fritos

1- 15 oz. can chili

Brown meat, add ¾ c. onion and celery. Cook until tender. Drain. Add pepper and chili and heat. Place layer of chips in an ungreased 1 ½ quart casserole. Alternate layers of chili mixture, chips and cheese. Top with remaining onions and cheese. Cover and bake at 350° for 10 minutes or until hot. This is great leftover, if there is any!

## Apricot Chicken

**(Serve with baked potatoes or rice pilaf and garlic green beans)**

1 cut-up fryer in 9x13 pan. Mix 1 package dry onion soup mix (I buy bulk, 1 package = ⅓ cup), 1 cup Thousand Island Dressing or Catalina Dressing, 1 ½ cup apricot preserves. Spread sauce evenly over chicken. Cover and bake 1 ½ hours at 350°.

## Homemade Corndogs

## (Serve with ketchup and mustard, of course!)

⅔ cup sugar

1 cup cornmeal

1 cup flour

2 t. baking powder

½ t. baking soda

½ t. salt

Mix ingredients and add: 2 eggs, 1 cup buttermilk or sour milk, ½ cup margarine, melted.

Spread in greased 9x13 pan. Evenly position 1 package hot dogs in mixture. Add cheese if desired. Bake at 375 degrees for 30 minutes.

## Slow-cooked Tri-tip, Pork or Beef in Tortillas

Place tri-tip in slow cooker. Cover with 1 cup salsa (or, 1 medium can of tomatoes with green chilies), and 1 large can black beans.

Cook until tender (6–8 hours.) Shred and place in flour tortillas with cheese and sour cream.

## Homemade Chicken Nuggets

**(My daughter's favorite and it's fun (and messy) to make together. Serve with mashed potatoes and corn.)**

2 cups crushed corn flakes

1 T. paprika

2 t. seasoned salt

¼ cup parmesan cheese

1 cup flour

½ cup buttermilk

6 boneless skinless chicken breast halves, cut in bite-sized pieces

2 T. butter, melted

In a shallow bowl, combine the first 4 ingredients. Place flour and buttermilk in separate shallow bowls. Coat chicken with flour, dip in buttermilk, then coat with corn flake mixture. Place on a greased 9x13 pan and drizzle with melted butter. Bake uncovered at 375 °F for 30–35 minutes or until browned.

# Hamburger Stroganoff

## (Serve on steamed rice or cooked pasta with broccoli (maybe!) on the side.)

1 lb. hamburger, browned and drained

1 can cream of mushroom soup

1 small can of sliced mushrooms or 1 cup of sliced fresh mushrooms

1 cup of sour cream

1 t. paprika

1 T. flour

1 t. salt

¼ t. pepper

Brown hamburger, add onion if desired. Add soup and mushrooms and cook gently for 15 minutes, stirring occasionally. Add flour and seasonings, stir. Stir in sour cream and heat without boiling.

# Leftovers Tonight

Often just two cups of leftovers are enough to feed a crowd the next night or week. Just add them to another savory dish. After a roast beef or chicken meal, bag up the leftover meat in two-cup portions and freeze for a later time. Next time you have unexpected company, or your pantry runs low before the paycheck comes in, you'll be pleasantly surprised with that extra bag of leftovers. Here are some favorite entrées that use up that last bit of another meal and give a delicious twist to "leftovers tonight!" And you may find yourself cooking "extra" just so you can make one of these specialties later on.

## After Thanksgiving Turkey Bake

### (leftover mashed potatoes, leftover chicken or turkey)

3 cups mashed potatoes

1 ½ -2 cups cooked chicken or turkey

1 can French Fried onions

1 cup shredded cheese

1 10oz. package frozen mixed vegetables (thawed, drained)

1 can cream of chicken soup

¼ cup milk

½ t. dry mustard

¼ t. garlic powder

¼ t. pepper

Combine potatoes, half of cheese, half of onions and spoon into 1 ½ qt. casserole. Mix remaining ingredients except cheese and onions. Pour into potato shell. Bake uncovered 30 minutes at 375 °F. Top with cheese/onions. Bake 3 minutes. Let stand 5 minutes before serving. Delish!

## Poppy Seed Chicken

### (leftover chicken/turkey; optional leftover rice)

Mix 3-4 cups of cooked shredded chicken or turkey with 1 can cream soup and 1 cup of sour cream. If using leftover rice, place rice in casserole and cover with chicken mixture; otherwise, simply place mixture in pan and cover with topping: a tube of crushed Ritz crackers or corn flakes mixed with a cube of melted butter and 1 teaspoon poppy seed. Bake until browned at 350 °F, 30–40 minutes.

## Chicken Tortilla Casserole

### (leftover chicken/turkey; serve with sliced fruit and warmed corn tortillas.)

3-4 cooked chicken breasts

12 corn tortillas

½ medium onion, diced

1 small can chopped green chilies

2 cups of grated Cheddar or Jack cheese

1 can cream of mushroom soup

1 can cream of chicken soup

1 can chicken broth

Mix soups and broth in a small bowl. In a greased 2- quart pan, layer tortillas, chicken, onion, chilies, and soup mixture, reserving most of the soup for the top. Sprinkle with cheese. Bake at 350° for approximately 45 minutes.

Alternative ingredients: If short on chicken, add 1 can of pinto beans, drained. Use just 1 can of cream soup, and after layering, pour over the top 1 can of mild green enchilada sauce. Cover with foil before baking.

## Spaghetti Pie

### (leftover pasta and spaghetti sauce)

Whenever you prepare a spaghetti dinner, make extra sauce and pasta. After dinner, mix about 1 cup of pasta with ¼ cup Parmesan cheese and 1 egg. Pour this mixture into a greased pie plate. Pour spaghetti sauce and meat onto the pasta "crust." Top with shredded mozzarella cheese. Cover with wrap and refrigerate or freeze. Later, defrost and bake until hot and bubbly. Use a disposable pie plate if you want to have a ready-made meal for a friend in need.

## Bacon Fried Rice

### (leftover rice and meat/vegetables)

½ lb. bacon

4 cups cold, cooked rice

3 eggs

½ t. salt

4 T. oil, divided

½ cup green onions, diced

4 T. soy sauce

any leftover chopped vegetables—Chinese cabbage is especially good (opt.)

Cut bacon into ¼ inch pieces, fry and drain. Beat eggs until well mixed, scramble with 1 T. oil, break into small bits and set aside. Heat 3 T. oil and add rice. Blend in soy sauce and salt. Add eggs, green onions, and bacon. Mix well. May be kept in warm oven covered for ½ hour.

## Baked Potato Soup

### (leftover baked potatoes)

⅔ cup butter or margarine

⅔ cup flour

7 cups milk (preferably whole)

6 large baking potatoes (baked, cooled, peeled and cubed, approximately 4 cups)

4 green onions, sliced

12 strips cooked and crumbled bacon

1 ¼ - 2 cups grated cheddar cheese

1 cup sour cream

¾ t. salt

½ t. pepper

In large pot, melt butter, stir in flour, heat and stir until smooth. Gradually add milk stirring constantly until thickened. Add potatoes and onions, bring to a boil, stirring constantly. Reduce heat, simmer for 10 minutes. Add the remaining ingredients, stir until cheese is melted. Yields 8 – 10 servings.

# What to Keep in Your Pantry (to make life easier)

"If you think you have to go to the store, you'll be less likely to invite someone over at the last minute." —Trish Larsen

The secret to not stressing out over last-minute company or what to serve a hungry crowd is knowing what you like and keeping the needed staples in your pantry. That doesn't assume you have a walk-in gourmet closet or basement shelves full of canned goods. It may just mean buying one extra can of beans or bag of flour when it's on sale. I've included a list of typical pantry items, but your pantry may have a whole different look.

Customize your cupboard to fit the things you like to cook for family and friends. I've added "Potential Options" under each category to give you an idea of how you might customize your pantry. Take a look at what your favorite recipes need and add their unique ingredients to your pantry. Allie includes hoisin sauce for specialty Chinese cooking, and now I keep it on hand, too, for Moo Shu What-You-Have. You may love Greek olives or artichoke hearts to jazz up a last-minute casserole or salad. Joanie always has block chocolate for those Monday afternoon chocolate coffees. I usually settle for dry cocoa. For last-minute desserts, you may want to keep a cake or brownie mix on hand, but it's up to your own style if you like the canned frosting or the homemade powdered sugar icing.

The point is this: Make your cupboard fit who you are—not me, not Joanie, not your mother. This section is to help you fill your pantry so that you will be ready to host, easily and conveniently. So fill it your way, but do try to fill it! You'll be happy you did when 6 ninth graders come over after practice for a bite to eat or you meet a family, new to town, who need a hot meal and a warm welcome.

## Staples:

cereals and oats

flour

baking powder, baking soda

corn starch

salt/pepper/spices

mayonnaise/mustards/ketchup

salad dressings

soy sauce

Worcestershire sauce

taco seasoning packets

sugar: white, brown, powdered

syrup

chocolate chips

dry cocoa/baking chocolate

nuts

birthday candles

cream soups

chicken broth (canned or granules)

pasta/rice/quinoa

vinegars

oils (olive, canola)

shortening

vanilla

cake mixes/brownie mix

*Possible Options*: cake flour, almond extract, poppy seeds, sesame seeds, molasses, hoisin sauce, hot pepper sauce, cooking wine, canned frosting, instant dry pudding, pizza sauce


**Bakery:**

bread/bagels/buns

crackers

tortillas (corn, flour)

*Possible Options*: pita bread, bread machine mixes, frozen bread dough loaves, pizza dough mix


**Beverages:**

frozen juice/lemonade

coffee/tea/herb teas

*Possible Options*: favorite sodas of kids' friends, chai tea, decaffeinated drinks

**Vegetables:**

fresh: salad
veggies/broccoli/carrots/mushrooms/potatoes/onions/garlic cloves

canned tomatoes

canned chili beans/baked beans/refried beans

canned mushrooms

olives

salsa

chop, bag, and freeze: onions/green pepper

frozen French fries/hash browns

frozen corn/peas/green beans/chopped spinach

*Possible Options:* garlic mashed potatoes (instant), black beans, taco sauce, dry beans, artichoke hearts (canned or frozen), French Fried onions


**Dairy:**

milk

butter/margarine

cream cheese/sour cream

yogurt

eggs

cheese (freeze shredded cheese in 3-cup portions)

ice cream/whipped toppings

*Possible Options*: chocolate syrup, instant chocolate milk powder, buttermilk

**Snacks/Kids:**

macaroni and cheese mixes

popcorn

peanut butter, jam

honey

graham crackers

*Possible Options*: cookies, canned refrigerator biscuits, cheese crackers, granola bars

**Meat:**

bacon/turkey sausage

ham

frozen chicken tenders (uncooked)

hamburger (cook, drain, pack in sandwich bags to freeze)

boneless, skinless chicken breasts

*Possible Options*: frozen chicken tenders (uncooked), turkey dogs, pepperoni slices

**Fruits:**

fresh in season

canned pineapple/oranges

applesauce

raisins

*Possible Options*: dried fruit (mangos, apples, cranberries)

 **TIP**: It's good to have one good neighbor from whom you feel free to borrow something at the last minute—a really good one will even lend you an extra house key!

My aunt serves the same dinner menu whenever she has Sunday company and it's always delicious – roast beef, carrots, potatoes and gravy. You might like more than one menu. Try out several and find one or two that suit you and your family best. Your guests won't mind if they get asked over more than once and find the same delicious entrée, salad, or dessert—or all three! One idea is to create a menu for a vegetarian meal, a budget meal, and a more high-priced meal. Then, practice all three so that you feel comfortable doing any of the three at any given time when the occasion presents itself. The main ingredient to hospitality is not the food, and the less stressed you are in serving what you have, the more you can focus on loving your guests.

We can all offer something. You may enjoy elaborate entrées with fancy sauces and stuffings. Another may prefer homemade banana splits or caramel corn. Once I dropped in on an old friend and she offered my kids root beer floats! I was impressed with her spontaneity, and the kids loved it. Work within your particular budget and time allotment and you will become more and more comfortable creating your personal style. Then watch God offer His welcome amidst the food, whatever you serve.

~~

# "K" Bars

1 cup sugar

1 cup white Karo syrup

1 ½ cups peanut butter

6 cups Special K cereal

1 package butterscotch chips

1 cup chocolate chips

In large pot, combine sugar and Karo syrup. Over a low flame, stir constantly until just under a boil. Remove from heat and stir in peanut butter and cereal. Spread in buttered 9x13 pan.

Icing: Over low heat or in microwave, melt butterscotch and chocolate chips together. Stir until smooth. Frost bars. When cool, cut into squares.

# Chapter 9

# Theme Gatherings to Lift the Spirit

## The Point is Relationships

I once saw a beautiful glossy photo that accompanied the following magazine ad:

"Welcome to The Gathering House, a barn home for the 1990s. This Yankee Barn post and beam frame--crafted from antique, reclaimed timbers--creates large open living areas and small intimate spaces for the modern extended family to gather."

I loved that. No, I don't need a barn, even one made from antique timbers. Still, it's a great thought. Gathering is the essence of a home. You may not want "The Gathering House" carved over your front door, but the idea needs to be engraved on your heart and mind.

Since God is all about loving people, the idea for any gathering is to foster relationships and create common bonds. What better place than our homes to show others that God loves a good belly laugh with the best of them? He longs to encourage every person He brings through your door, whether your daughter's basketball team swarms your sofa (and chairs and floor), or the table is set with an extra cup for you and a new neighbor to get better acquainted.

You may want to be hospitable, but you're not sure about how to begin. Theme Gatherings can help both the host and the guest. Using a central idea provides the courage to get started and can even get the most shy or self-conscious person to step over your threshold. You won't need to worry about conversation starters when you invite friends (or strangers) to your "Tacky Party." Guests will be talking about the funky costumes, the duct tape on the linoleum or the fact that you left the sprinkler going out in front, with guests arriving just a little damp.

Twenty-five Theme Gathering ideas are included in this chapter. Three of my favorites are described at length at the beginning so you get the idea of how God can use them to create special bonds between people and Himself. Maybe you've already done one or two on the list with your own special twist. As you read along, you may think of something different you could do that fits your style and home. This list is to show you that sometimes a simple idea can make all the difference in making someone experience the warmth and reality of God's welcome.

## Three Parties with a Purpose

### 1. The God-Is-Faithful Party

Tim and Leslie, after months of praying and looking for God's direction, decided it was time to move out-of-state. All those who knew and loved them recognized this decision was coming eventually, but it was a little hard on us. I asked to give them a "Good-bye party," but Tim wasn't so sure he wanted all that attention and spotlight, even for just one night. He just kept saying, "You know, it's all about God and how faithful He's been to us." So that's how a "Farewell Party" turned into a "God Is Faithful Party"; and what a wonderful time of celebration and remembrance it turned out to be. The invitation read:

"Bring something that reminds you of a time that God was faithful—to celebrate God's faithfulness to our dear friends, Tim and Leslie Crocker."

After appetizers, thirty-five people or so stood, one after and another, doing a "show and tell." They presented their item and described how it represented God's blessing. One man showed his wristwatch, explaining that his beloved wife had been given only ten years to live, fifteen years earlier, and she was alive and well and by his side. God had given them *time* together, more than they had hoped for. A woman wore her wedding veil to symbolize God's faithfulness in bringing her a husband late in life. We cried and laughed, and of course, spoke often of how the Crockers had been faithful friends to us. God got the attention, we delighted in each other's stories, and Tim and Leslie felt loved and encouraged.

## 2. Bean Auction

Whether you are the new kid on the block, or a new family or two have recently joined your neighborhood, a fun way to get acquainted is to host a "Bean Auction." A crowd is best for this hilarious game that ends with a surprise twist. Since it's "beans" we're talking about, the dress (or costume) is casual (farm clothes?) and bean dip can be on the menu. Potluck the appetizers and provide hot fudge sundaes at the end of the evening.

As the guests arrive, present each with a grab bag of dry beans with the simple instruction: "Take some." (Your kids may like to help with this part.) Guests choose how many beans but no explanation is given. Provide them with a baggie in which to keep them. Next, the guests fill out a slip of paper that reads: "What activity would you be willing to host or participate in with another person, family or couple?" Keep it under $25. (Examples include: a kite-flying picnic in the park; homemade fried chicken dinner; berry or apple picking; pie and coffee at a local hang out; BBQ-ing and a movie.) These slips go into a large jar or bowl.

Choose an outgoing friend to be the "auctioneer" and gather your crowd. We used a wooden meat tenderizer for the gavel, and the party began. The auctioneer chooses an activity from the jar and reads it off without divulging the name on the paper. He proceeds to auction off the activity, while guests bid with their beans. The surprise: the more beans you took at the beginning, the better off you are! Woe to the guest who chose only three beans; he is outbid until the end! Each activity is claimed by the highest bidder, who then finds out who is hosting his prized event. The rule is to fulfill the claim within three months. After a loud bidding period, dessert is served and dates are set up to get together in the days and weeks ahead. This fun gathering is simple to carry out and includes a bonus: the gift of future gatherings as couples and families team up to enjoy their outing together.

## 3. Birthday Party for Jesus

One December, I asked my friend Debbi to pray that I would know what to give the Lord Jesus for His birthday. A week before Christmas, I had girlfriends over for leftover corn sausage chowder. The discussion turned to what we could do in our kids' classrooms to spread true Christmas cheer. Debbi turned to me and said, "I know what your present to Jesus is supposed to be!"

"I just gave it," I replied, "you are all here for lunch!" She ignored me: "You are supposed to invite all the kids in Bonnie's kindergarten class for a birthday party for Jesus, and I'll help."

We ended up inviting all the girls in my daughter's class. Eleven came, and a twelve-year tradition was born in the Donaldson home. Every year things were done a little differently, but key elements included birthday cake or cupcakes, a Christmas craft, and a story. We have used flannel graph, storybooks on a Christmas theme and a picture book of the nativity. I'm "craft-impaired" myself, so I was always blessed to have creative friends to run that activity. Some years it was all about glitter; other years it was popcorn paper plate wreaths or stamp art cards and gift tags. As our family grew, so did the age span and number of guests. Often, twenty-five kids arrived, ranging from age 5 to 14. Since we celebrated Jesus' birthday, we would invite the guests to bring Him a gift: baby clothing or toys, new or gently used, unwrapped, which we donated to a local crisis pregnancy center. The climax came when we lighted candles on each cupcake and the kids sang the Guest of Honor a rousing chorus of "Happy Birthday!" When the last child was picked up and the floor was covered with sequins and construction paper, we knew the holy season had begun (or ended) well.

For some children, the "Birthday Party for Jesus" is their first introduction to the real meaning of Christmas, and you, as the host, can know that Jesus is pleased with your gift.

# More Gatherings Around a Theme

## 4. Chocolate Open House

A great idea for a group that doesn't know each other very well, e.g., neighbors or work colleagues. Guests are invited to bring something chocolate; the host provides several items such as chocolate truffles and hot fudge sauce for fruit dipping, as well as strong coffee and ice water. Good for Christmas— someone can make a chocolate Birthday cake* for the Baby Jesus.

## 5. Midwestern Potluck

Bring any entrée made with cream of mushroom soup and one side dish of Jell-O or deviled eggs. The hosts provide tapioca pudding and bar cookies. Women wear bib aprons, men wear suspenders; guests "interview" each other and introduce someone to the group. It's fun to guess what kind of seed packet is pinned to your back as you do the interviewing. End the evening with a wild game of Bunko or Pictionary.

## 6. Recession Party

Wear something you've had in your closet longer than 5 years, serve "Stone Soup"—each guest brings something to put in the soup; the hostess provides the broth and serves cornbread. This can also be **Tacky Party Potluck.** Prizes can be awarded for the tackiest outfits and entrées. Spam and marshmallow Jell-O usually win out! These are great times for the whole family to be included, especially if you include a tacky talent show.

## 7. Waffle Night

Guests bring toppings; you may need to borrow extra waffle irons. This party works well after a business or church meeting, especially if sliced apples and cinnamon have been simmering in your crockpot all day.

## 8. Park Walk

Have everyone meet at your house, and bring picnic basket food. As you walk, assign partners for people to talk with on the way there; then, during the watermelon feasting, each person "introduces" his or her partner to the rest of the group with information gleaned from their conversation.

## 9. Retreat-in-a-Basket

Everyone brings a basket of favorite goodies to exchange with another guest; draw names to make the exchanges. Each person shares what brings her "retreat" after a stressful day.

## 10. Give Yourself a Kitchen Shower

We all need new towels or measuring cups after ten or more years of marriage. Everyone buys herself something new—under $25—and brings it wrapped and tagged for her. Then, each lady gets to open her own present amidst the oohs! and ahs! of her friends. End with lemon pie and a devotional to encourage everyone in their homemaking.

## 11. Cookie Night/Afternoon

Whole families can be included. Choose 3 recipes, create cookie-making "stations" around the house; take turns if space is limited. Sample some cookies, bag the rest for friends, church staff, or the elderly; deliver as a family. This is a great icebreaker with a mixed group of strangers.

## 12. Greatest Vacations Night

Each guest or family dresses in their vacation outfit, brings a limited number of vacation photos, and comes prepared to tell one outrageous story about their favorite trip, true or otherwise. The guests have to guess which parts are true or not.

## 13. "Power Brunch" for Christmas Shoppers

Make it early on a Saturday morning, invite neighbors you might not see very often due to work schedules. Everyone brings a "tip" to share for making the season less stressful; pass out goodie bags filled with aspirin, chocolate kisses, and a Christmas verse.

## 14. Pizza Night

Provide the English muffins and spaghetti sauce. Guests bring pizza toppings and stack their own personal mini-pizzas; play a rousing game of Pictionary, round-robin UNO, or Trivial Pursuit. **Burrito Night/Baked Potato Feast** (Same idea: guests bring toppings. Host provides the tortillas or potatoes and beverage.

## 15. Fascinating Friends Gathering

Invite people who don't necessarily know one another, but who are "interesting" in their own right and provide a unique contribution to your life. You, as the host, say a little about each person and give them an opportunity to say how they developed their gift or interest. If one of the interests is music, then have that friend lead a sing-along or provide a short concert. It's a great way to celebrate God's special creativity in making us all so different and reflective of His beauty.

## 16. Mug Night

Bring a favorite mug. Everything is served in the same mug: chili, beverage, ice cream sundaes. Yes, guests can wash them out between courses. Everyone bring a baby picture ("mug shot") and people guess who's who.

## 17. Christmas in July

Decorate for Christmas—string lights on a houseplant. Find out what a missionary family could use. Everyone brings gifts for that family unwrapped and wraps them one-by-one. Videotape the activity to send along with the gifts. Don't forget the caroling. Take donations for postage; provide boxes and brown paper for overseas shipping.

## 18. Chinese Dinner

Decide on three entrées. Guests bring veggies. Take turns at the chopping board and wok, and reading the directions. Men like the stopwatch/timer and giving the instructions. Try a Chinese egg soup, to be prepared in advance, and guests can indulge while the stir-frying is going on. There's nothing like close fellowship in the kitchen, and afterwards everyone can write fortunes for each other.

### 19. Outdoor Party-athon

Provide croquet, badminton, and Ping Pong, and design a simple obstacle course. Winners move on to the next activity after a short period or the game is over. End with a watermelon feed and give prizes to all participants. Use the park if your yard is too small.

### 20. "Bobby Crocker Cook-off"

Men bring their homemade entrées or goodies; women sample and judge. The judging and the eating is the entertainment.

### 21. Mystery Night

Come dressed as a detective, watch *Death on the Nile* or tell a round-robin story, each person continuing the story when a bell rings.

### 22. Birthday Blessing Coffee

Guests bring something that will bless the birthday person, e.g., a verse, a quote, a card, a gift, and present it to her while expressing how she has been a blessing to them. The honored guest will never forget it. And be sure to pass the tissue box.

## 23. Mothers-of-your-kids'-friends Salad Potluck

Send flyer home with kids in your child's class—with the teacher's permission. All moms bring a salad. You provide the beverage, bread and dessert. A great way to make new friends and open your home.

## 24. "New Leaf Luncheon"

This is a great way to start a new year. Everyone brings an idea for a New Year's resolution, as in "turning over a new leaf." They also have the option to share an organizational tip. Guests write down their ideas on leaf-shaped paper or on real leaves; after they are all shared, pray for each other for the new year God has given you.

## 25. "I Can Read!"

Celebrate a child who has learned to read. Make potato print placemats on newsprint as a craft. Stack favorite books for your centerpiece. Invite special friends to bring their favorite book to share. The highlight comes from reading letters written by favorite aunts or grandmothers or teachers expressing their own love of books and celebrating your child's new accomplishment.

~~

# Trishie's Apple Crisp

5 large apples

1 t. cinnamon

¼ t. nutmeg

1 t. lemon juice

½ c. water

1 c. sugar

¾ c. flour

½ c. butter

Peel and slice apples into a buttered 8x11 baking dish, sprinkle with spices and add lemon juice and water.

Mix the sugar and flour and work in the butter to make a crumbly mixture. Spread on top to cover apples. Bake at 350° for 1 hour. Serve with vanilla ice cream, of course!

# Chapter 10

# Your Home . . . His Heart

My friend asked me: "Are we all 'called' to be hospitable?"

I knew she wanted me to say, "No."

She went on: "Sue, think about it. If you just LOVE swimming, but I am afraid of water, how would you convince me that our bodies were intended to swim, and that to not swim—because of fear—would be to cut off an opportunity to use our bodies for God, maybe even saving someone's life?"

I loved her analogy. She's not the only one afraid of the water. God may not have intended us to swim, but He did intend for us to host for His sake. And the great thing is, we *do* have the chance to save a person's life. A simple cup of coffee can be a first step in inviting that friend to the Ultimate Host.

Being God's welcome to our world is the heart of hospitality. It's not how many we invite or what food we serve, the number of bathrooms in our house or the size of our television. When we make Christ our centerpiece, all other details fall into place.

Do you need to be taught to swim? I hope these pages have gotten you to the edge of the pool and encouraged you to get your feet wet, maybe even take a few laps.

Perhaps you've been swimming a long time but didn't know why. And now that you know that when you swim, you are more like Jesus, or that swimming easily across the pool helps others know who Jesus is, you are motivated even more to keep up your strokes.

Maybe you've gotten out of the habit, and now it's time to get wet again for the Kingdom's sake. Your friends and contacts have changed over the years, and God wants to begin using you and your home again to draw others to Himself.

You need to be reminded that you already know how to be hospitable, if you just relax and be yourself. The best hostess presents the gift of herself, accepting and loving the guest at her table. Somewhere along the way, someone may have gotten the message that God is unapproachable. He's too big, too vague, too harsh, too impersonal. Then, you come into her life and show her His welcoming heart. Nothing to lose, and everything to gain.

Hospitality is about the guest. The host reaches out, risks failure, and trusts God with the outcome.

My sister Lori said she made great efforts with her Japanese friend. The language was a huge barrier. Yuka eventually RSVP'd to God's invitation to know Him personally, but it all started with lunch and a prayer and sharing recipes—lots of flipping through recipes. Lori took the plunge and kept swimming, and another life was saved.

Jeanine MacLachlan, in her book *The Rustic Kitchen* said:

"When you entertain, don't do anything that makes you stressed. Your guests would rather relax and have fun than feel that they've put you out."

I love that. Remember to breathe, jump in and see how God uses you and your table set for more than one.

## The Invitation House: What It Takes

I drove by a beautiful Asian restaurant called The Invitation House. What a great name for a Japanese/Korean restaurant. Both Japanese and Korean cultures are extremely hospitable. My friends Helen and Mika love to have me over for dinner and feed me until I burst. They each could post that same sign: "The Invitation House."

Maybe we don't need a plaque on our porch that reads, "The Invitation House," but we may need to examine what sign is currently hanging there. It'd be so great to see this one: "I know God welcomed me, so now I will welcome you."

What sign do you have out front? Sign or no sign, hospitable homes look different on the outside but the heart of each home is the same: "You're welcome here. Come on in. We're so glad you came."

What does it take to change your front porch shingle from "The Closed House," "The Unfriendly House," or "The Hesitant House" to "The Welcoming House"? No matter how many times I've invited people over, I still find that hospitality takes courage, cooperation, and commitment.

## Hospitality Takes Courage

I didn't have room in this book to describe all the "turkey failures" at Thanksgiving that friends have shared with me. Someone told me once that cooking a turkey was so easy, but not so according to my friends Laurie, Cathy and Karen. Their hilarious stories are now the stuff of family legend, but it wasn't funny at the time. Either the turkey wasn't defrosted in time or it came out burned on the outside and raw in the middle. One friend ended up cutting up the raw bird and microwaving the pieces. It's not as if the turkey wasn't the main entrée--it was Thanksgiving, for heaven's sake!

Mistakes can turn out to be the best teachers, after all. When our kids see us ruin a casserole and live to laugh about it while we go to plan B, they learn how to handle pressure with grace. Best of all, they learn that the guests don't mind as they help you make do with what you have.

In spite of any short-term personal humiliation, I've found that there are so many benefits to making mistakes that it's worth the plunge for that reason alone. We fear failure more when we're younger and less experienced. That's because when we're older, we've failed a few times already and have not died and gone to heaven on the spot. The party and life does go on.

God continues to use my "failures" in life to remind me of good things like:

~ He's in control

~ I'm doing it for Him

~I'm being too proud

~It's the guest that's important, not my reputation

~He loves me for who I am, not for what I do

~I can make others feel at ease.

A great benefit to failure is that you find out you're not alone—everyone has failed a time or two. Your guests can identify more with "less than perfection." They aren't perfect either, and when they observe your faux pas, it makes them feel at ease. If a new friend came over and experienced perfection at your table, how would she feel about inviting you or anyone else over? Our blunders give others a great gift: the permission to be themselves.

We had the pastor and his wife for dinner after we had been married a month. I changed the recipe "just a little" and the meatloaf came out raw in the middle, which I didn't discover until after I had served it. The whole time I was reheating each plate in the microwave and sweating like crazy, dear Doris, our pastor's wife, was telling us a story about the time she had tried to bake a stewing chicken for Sunday company. Their friends ended up taking them out for dinner! I wasn't sure what a stewing chicken was, but I was so glad she kept talking. I wasn't the only one to make a food fiasco.

Mistakes are okay because people are just happy to be invited; they don't want everything to be perfect, because they aren't perfect.

Another benefit is that through our perceived failures, we learn to depend on God. If things are too easy, we forgot how much we need Him. He's the center of our welcome table, but we can forget Him altogether in the hustle and bustle of making everything turn out just right.

Living near a large university, my sister's family often invited groups of foreign students to their home. It wasn't always a success. She told me this story:    "One of the first, maybe THE first, foreign student party we had in the condo in Austin was one of the worst. All the students were new to me but one. I seem to remember that they were all quiet Asians who just sat around the living room in chairs and didn't talk much. I HATE silence at a party. My toes crinkle even now as I remember Leonard [Lori's husband] valiantly trying to get conversations going with somewhat unresponsive guests. Maybe they were unsure of how they were supposed to act, I don't know, but I remember it as painful. After that, I said, "Never again!" and determined to have board games out and my kids ready to man them. The next event was full of lots of UNO and Clue and laughter. However, one must note a VERY important caveat: at that first painful party, we made friends with a charming man from Singapore named Weisun. From that contact, we invited him over for dinner another time. From that private dinner sprang amazing conversation, which later led to his conversion and joining our church in Austin, marrying another Christian foreign student from our church and having a big family. They are still in Austin, and I hear from them now and then. So, even the perceived failures are not necessarily so in God's plan. My advice is to keep on going and let God do what He wants with it all. But do keep the UNO cards handy, especially for foreigners!"

Lori learned a great lesson. Her party wasn't her favorite; it was fairly painful, in fact. But God used it for His kingdom, and she continued to take risks in spite of "perceived failure" and personal discomfort. Her "never again" became "Okay, I'll try it again, anyway." That takes courage and a desire to please God. And Weisun became a member of God's family.

When my party malfunctions, I am reminded that I work and live and host for an Audience of One. When the soup flops and our faces get hot with embarrassment, God still gets His work done, and it's not just our guests who are changed. Humble pie may be what He wants on our menu rather than Tiramisu or Crème Brule. And, He gives the courage to try again.

## Hospitality Takes Cooperation

My friend Judy didn't grow up in a hospitable home, but her husband did. They overcame their different backgrounds, and the fact that they both worked full-time by developing "no brainer" menus. Their favorite: Tri-tip, peas, Rice-a-Roni and bread. Joe BBQ'd the beef and Judy did the rest.

Hospitality was easy for Joe, and Judy could pitch in and overcome her discomfort because they used a tried-and-true formula that gave her the confidence to concentrate on their guests.

Unless it's a ladies' coffee in the middle of the day, most of hospitality takes the cooperation of the whole family. To help each of the family members get on the same page, talk with your husband, kids, or housemates about God's hospitality and yours. Here are some good issues to cover:

1. How important is our hospitality in God's eyes?

2. What did hospitality look like in your home growing up?

3. What things were different between you and your spouse or roommates?

4. What is the best way for your family to deliver hospitality to others? Do weekends work better? Is spontaneity comfortable for everyone? (If not, be spontaneous every other time or only when it won't intrude on another's schedule.) Do we plan a certain day of the month or week to automatically have company?

If these questions are covered, things run more smoothly, family members will be more willing to pitch in, and the most opposite backgrounds can begin to blend, for Jesus' sake.

Even a child can understand an explanation of God's welcome heart. As your son or daughter helps you plan a play date with a buddy, remind him or her that God invited us first to spend time with Him, and He is the best friend we can have. We aren't put here on earth just to have fun or to be entertained. Point out how bringing someone into your home is a way to share God's friendship.

When my third grader began mentioning forming little clubs with girls at school, I told her that we could start our own club with her friends during the summer. We called it the "Summer Fun Son Club" and ran it for three summers, for five weeks. The idea was to have fun and have it centered around the Son, Jesus Christ. We made dinner for the families, created a front yard Olympics, and took sign language lessons from a neighbor. Hosting became comfortable for our girls as they invited their friends in each week, and we had a chance to share Jesus through Bible stories and relationships. They learned purpose-filled hospitality, and in the meantime, they had a great summer.

Family dynamics are always changing, and we need to stay flexible in our expectations of what each family member can contribute or endure. Mark prefers company on a Saturday night, because he's too bushed on Friday after a full week of work. But we can still fit in single girlfriends or our kids' friends any night of the week that the kids are home and we have an extra portion to share.

One discussion I continue to have with my patient husband is: "Should we have a crowd, or just one?" I love a crowd because I have to clean the house just as much for one person as I do for three families. I like the noise and the camaraderie—it's more like a party, and I love a good party (like my sister!) My darling, introverted and very wise husband prefers getting acquainted with one or two people at a time. "You dilute the fellowship with too many people," he's counseled on more than one occasion. And he's right (darn it!) It is easier to go deeper with fewer guests. So, sometimes we invite the neighbors, and sometimes we invite *one* neighbor, and we've both come to value the other's preference. Our cooperation didn't happen overnight, and we still don't always get it right. But it helps to bring our differences to the table even as we bring our guests, for the sake of the Kingdom.

## Hospitality Takes Commitment

Why is commitment so important? It's because hospitality is work and love combined. And sometimes it's so much work that it helps to remember how much we love God and that's really why we do it. Someone told me, "I've worn myself out serving others, but they all seemed to have a blast. [Hospitality] is not about me. That is the key."

Oswald Chamber wrote, in his devotional *My Utmost for His Highest*: "Don't testify how much you love Me . . . but 'feed my sheep.' And there are some extraordinarily funny sheep . . .'"

Paula's passion is to feed the world. She takes hospitality on the road. When Terri and Frank's daughter was diagnosed with cancer, Paula and a friend took dinner to their family every Monday night for a year—and Frank is a vegetarian, a challenge that Paula took to heart as she explored new recipes. She is the first one to offer a meal when someone needs a boost. It's her way of loving and caring, and it takes time and preparation and effort.

Unless you have a full-time maid and cook, it must be said that hospitality isn't always easy. Planning helps, but there is still the physical labor, the time, and money.

My mom told me about her friend who hosts with panache and elegance. "Sue, you wouldn't believe how beautiful everything is. She uses the best china and napkins, and the food is out of this world. Use her for your book." I went on to discover that this glorious friend also had a housekeeper and would hire extra cooks and waiters for her dinner parties. This impressed my mom, that's for certain, but it's not the topic of this book. If this were what hospitality was about, only the wealthy could do it right without going into cardiac arrest or early admission into a rest home. I'm sure my sign out front after any major event would read: "Stay away. Hostess recovering for next 8 months."

A friend of mine invited the college group for dinner and was told to expect 15 to 20 students. Instead, 30 showed up because one young man had 10 friends who were visiting, so he brought them all! (Don't you just love college kids?) This wasn't exactly convenient, but God provided. There wasn't even a bite left over, but there was enough.

Quinn Sherrer wrote, in her book *The Warm and Welcoming Home*: "I wonder if Martha felt it was inconvenient to have Jesus come for dinner because He was always bringing 12 extra people along with Him, known as the disciples."

Of course, it's always fun to get tons of compliments and heartfelt gratitude from any of our guests. But a thank-you doesn't always outweigh the effort or inconvenience, and sometimes it never arrives.

Hospitality takes work, and it may be inconvenient, but we don't do the work so that we can impress someone or look for repayment. The purpose is so that others can know that God has made them welcome at His table. And that welcome can happen on the living room floor on a blanket with popcorn and apple cider, even if the popcorn runs out and the cider gets spilled on the carpet.

Everyone needs water, but not everyone is thirsty. The woman at the well was seeking. She blustered around a bit, but when she recognized life behind Christ's words, "Here's My Living Water" she accepted His invitation. Our job is to prime the pump and pour the water, and never stop.

Pray for parched throats. And, for yourself, pray for perseverance.

Sometimes we have a rollicking good time in being hospitable, with everyone helping in the kitchen until the work is done. And sometimes not. But that's not really the point, is it?

## Embracing God's Welcome

Someone wrote: "To come home is to put yourself with those who put yourself at ease."

As I write this, our home is being remodeled. It's torn up from top to bottom. We're cold, dust is everywhere, and mice brazenly set up housekeeping in most walls. But, it's still our refuge and retreat, especially when the space heaters are on full blast. We're "at ease" most of the time when at home.

What if you don't have such a home? Your walls are in place (and they don't have mice), but you are not in a place of refuge and peace? Your life is a mess. You don't feel at home anywhere.

The psalmist wrote about what to do when we feel that way. He found his rest and ease with God, so he could always feel "at home." Psalm 71:3 in *THE MESSAGE* reads:

"I run for dear life to God, get me out of this mess. Be a guest room where I can retreat; You said Your door was always open. You're my salvation, my granite fortress."

Do I feel welcome at God's table? Do I run to His guest room and know I'm at home? Have I experienced His forgiveness, His acceptance, His rest?

A perfect home and gourmet cooking have little to do with hospitality. Knowing that God invites us to His guest room does. And once we're in, we keep the door open for anyone He brings our way.

True hospitality begins with this perspective:

God welcomed me. He is my true home. So now I will welcome others. Then they can meet Him, too.

In his book *Heaven*, Randy Alcorn wrote, "We are a displaced people longing for our true Home. . . . God who commands hospitality will not be outdone in His Hospitality to us."

There is no one more hospitable than God. We are privileged to reflect His welcoming heart to the world. God wants to use our hospitality as a vehicle to change lives.

If we are hesitant to welcome another, is it possible that it's because we just can't quite believe that we've been fully accepted? You can have that confidence. The Bible says: "In Him and through faith in Him we may approach God with freedom and confidence" (Ephesians 3:12).

Oswald Chambers wrote, in *My Utmost for His Highest*: ". . .all the time God has stood with outstretched hands, not only to take you, but for you to take Him."

## Becoming God's Welcome—Living the Gospel of Hospitality

Paul told us that God has given us a great job: "the ministry of reconciliation" (2 Corinthians 5:18,20). One way to go about that is in our homes. You meet someone new and think: *Wow, here's someone new. Let's invite him over. He may not know Jesus yet.*

My friend, Katy, said, "Sue, people may not remember what you said, or what you did, but they will remember how you made them feel."

Isn't that great?

Because God forgives, we forgive. Because we have intimacy with God, we can show others they can as well. Because we live in God's presence, we can invite our neighbor to join us.

Do we accept our role as God's personal greeter?

"Debbie, how are you? Have you met Jesus? Come on it, here He is. Let's have tea."

With Jesus by our side, we can open our door—front or back— —and call out, "Come on in! You're welcome here!"

We live in an automatic garage door world. People drive home and into their garages, and we never have to see each other. Sure, we might wave or maybe offer a few words of greeting and "How's the weather?" but not much beyond the civil word or polite greeting. It's all a front porch relationship, more like front sidewalk if you happen to be out watering or trimming hedges. Or maybe that's a hired gardener who doesn't even know your neighbor.

So how do we get beyond the sidewalk and the smoothly closing garage door?

We invite them in. We take the risk of knocking on their door. We exchange phone numbers and ask, "Can you come for hamburgers on Saturday?" We might feel funny. We might wish we could keep it as is: strangers—friendly strangers, true, but with no natural opportunity to find out who each other really is; no contact beyond the friendly wave. Are we only known as the family who drives out to church every Sunday morning? Is that as much as they know about Jesus?

Ask God to help you see the world, your neighborhood, as He sees it. And begin knocking.

How is your hospitality like God's? Can you even compare it?

How does one invite someone to life? We don't forgive sins, not the last time I checked. Our water might be crystal clear, but it's not the eternal variety. Our couch and table offer rest and nourishment, but it's only temporary.

So we welcome like God welcomes when we introduce our guests to Jesus. When we bring them to Jesus by the way we serve them, by the way we love them, by letting them know that God loves them no matter what they've done or where they've been. We don't forgive their sins, but we know the Forgiver, and we make the introductions.

There's nothing that makes us feel more welcome and loved than open arms, a loving smile and the words: "Come." "Come in and rest. You look tired." "Come in and have some tea."

"Come into the light and get a better look at what you're seeking. Come and have some more of me," Jesus says.

He says this to us on a daily basis. And He wants to say it through us to those around us. What fun—what a privilege—to be God's invitation to those who don't yet have the pleasure of His company.

~~

# Chocolate Chip Bars

⅔ cup shortening

1 cup sugar

1 t. salt

4 t. water

2 eggs

1 cup coconut (optional)

1 cup chocolate chips

1 cup brown sugar

2 cups flour

2 ½ t. baking powder

2 t. vanilla

Melt shortening in saucepan, remove from heat, add sugars and mix; add eggs; add dry ingredients last with coconut and chips. Bake in large cake pan at 350° for about 25 minutes. Cool and slice.

# The Favor of a Reply Is Requested

## The Invitation

"How blessed is the one whom You choose and bring near to You to dwell in Your courts. We will be satisfied with the goodness of Your house."

(Psalm 65:4, NIV)

"Won't you accept My invitation to My house? You'll find all you need and more. Here's what My Son said. Listen closely:

'God is not a secret to be kept. . . . Keep open house; be generous with your lives. By opening up to others, you'll prompt people to open up with God . . .'"
(Matthew 5:14,16, THE MESSAGE)

# The RSVP

Lord,

I accept. Thanks for inviting me into Your home. You are more than enough. Now I want to make my home an open house for You. I'm not sure how or when or who. But You do. You just want my willing heart. Okay, Lord, I'm all Yours. Where do I begin?

Write *your* RSVP:

For more recipes, hospitality tips, and inspiration,

subscribe to:

**Food For Body and Soul**

www.welcomeheart.com

I would love to hear your stories of hospitality—recipes, ideas, and where you are in the process of hosting for Heaven's sake.